The Psychology Student Writer's Manual and Reader's Guide

Third Edition

Jill M. Scott

University of Central Oklahoma Emeritus

Gregory M. Scott

University of Central Oklahoma Emeritus

Stephen M. Garrison

University of Central Oklahoma

ROWMAN & LITTLEFIELD

Lanham • *Boulder* • *New York* • *London*

Executive Editor: *Nancy Roberts*
Assistant Editor: *Megan Manzano*
Senior Marketing Manager: *Kim Lyons*
Interior Designer: *Ilze Lemesis*
Cover Designer: *Sally Rinehart*

Published by Rowman & Littlefield
An imprint of The Rowman & Littlefield Publishing Group, Inc.
4501 Forbes Boulevard, Suite 200, Lanham, Maryland 20706
www.rowman.com

Unit A, Whitacre Mews, 26-34 Stannary Street, London SE11 4AB, United Kingdom

British Library Cataloguing in Publication Information Available

Library of Congress Cataloging-in-Publication Data Available

ISBN 978-1-4422-6698-8 (hardcover : alk. paper)
ISBN 978-1-4422-6699-5 (pbk. : alk. paper)
ISBN 978-1-4422-6700-8 (ebook)

∞ ™ The paper used in this publication meets the minimum requirements of American National Standard for Information Sciences—Permanence of Paper for Printed Library Materials, ANSI/NISO Z39.48-1992.

Printed in the United States of America

BRIEF CONTENTS

CONTENTS

TO THE STUDENT

WELCOME TO A COMMUNITY OF SKILLED OBSERVERS AND HELPERS

One of the most successful books in psychology on personal problem-solving and developing opportunities is *The Skilled Helper* by Gerard Egan (10th ed., 2013). The title's elegant simplicity immediately directs students' attention to the essence of empowerment to take action that leads to effective results of their own choosing. It presents a framework for conceptualizing how to hear others in order to advance empathy, respect, and genuineness—in other words, to listen actively.

And so we invite you to join something similar: a community of *skilled observers*. This community is now, in 2018, officially 2,367 years old. That is because the seminal foundational work of psychology, Aristotle's (384–322 BCE) *De Anima* (On the Soul), was written in 350 BCE. It contains ideas that are foundational to the study of, for example, the mind and nervous system, the idea of souls, and basic ideas that Sigmund Freud applied to his developing theories of psychoanalysis. Aristotle articulated concepts that Freud interpolated, for example, libido, ego, id, and even the notion of self-actualization. But it is reasonable to claim that psychology as science—indeed all science—was born when, in *Politics*, Aristotle began his analysis of human behavior with the words **"observation shows us . . ."** With these three profound words, science as observation was established. Aristotle then proceeded to observe human potential around him as well as the potential and vitality of the plants and animals in the natural world. He chronicled the natural and human worlds of previous centuries. Aristotle recommended psychological considerations for the future, such as the notions of individual capacities and faculties, perception, nutrition, individual differences, and the criminal in society. For thousands of years now, understanding of psychological phenomena has been based upon skilled observation of human behavior. Today the multiple fields of psychology utilize scientific methodologies to augment how we measure what we see.

The academic discipline of psychology as we know it today, however, grew from the enthusiasm of William James at Harvard in the latter years of the 1800s. The American Psychological Association (APA) was launched in 1892 to organize a rapidly growing professional identity. A century of academic growth brought the advancement of the field of scientific psychology to establish its niche in 1988 with the Association for Psychological Science (APS).

Today psychologists study a wide variety of topics, perhaps best illustrated by the APA's and APS's lists of organized divisions of the discipline and journals. Turn for a moment to the references at the end of this volume to get an idea of the almost bewildering variety of subject matter studied by today's psychologists. As you peruse this list, you will see from the breadth of topics that the discipline of psychology offers myriad opportunities to study human behavior.

We shall make two final notes about this ancient as well as new discipline. First, its accomplishments outside academia are generally a little frightening and misunderstood. Many adults in the early 1900s were skeptical, even cynical, of the idea of just talking about emotional illness or about people who had distressing mental health behaviors. But humanity moved on. Everyone is familiar with the self-help era (Dear Abby, Dr. Spock, Norman Vincent Peale). This genus of practical psychology created in the United States a kinder, gentler face for the new discipline.

Second, Americans are little aware of the enormous influence psychological scientists continue to have on our lives, which is in some ways foundationally different from what things were like a century ago. The best examples might be in the identification and treatment of severe mental illness. Where did these techniques come from? In almost 120 years of modern academic and scientific psychology, the field is doing what science does best: careful observation, a clear hypothesis, and replicability, in addition to being open to influence from the disciplines of evolution, biology, sociology, physiology, and neurology. Before the 1900s (don't forget Aristotle), psychologists and scientists began studies to understand human behavior, and now, decades later, their continuing efforts and insights are employed in highly sophisticated ways for practical effect.

TO THE TEACHER

WHAT'S NEW IN THE THIRD EDITION?

While at times today's world appears to be an uninterrupted stream of reinvention, some things change slowly, if at all. That is why this book's primary value to you, the teacher, has remained the same for more than two decades. This book helps in dealing with three problems commonly faced by teachers of psychology:

1. Students increasingly need specific directions to produce a good paper.
2. Psychologists, as always, want to teach psychology, not English.
3. Students do not yet understand how and why to avoid plagiarism.

How many times have you assigned papers in your psychology classes and found yourself teaching the basics of writing—not only in terms of content but form and grammar as well? This text, which may either accompany the primary text you assign in any class or stand on its own, allows you to assign one of the types of papers described in parts 2 and 3, with the knowledge that virtually everything the student needs to know, from grammar to sources of information to reference style, is in part 1 of this one volume.

What's new in *The Psychology Student Writer's Manual and Reader's Guide, Third Edition*? Every chapter and chapter section has been updated and revised, many substantially. The following chapter sections are new in this edition:

1.1 Reading Psychology Analytically
1.2 Reading News as Interpersonal Influence
4.1 Psychodynamic
4.2 Behaviorist
4.3 Cognitive
5.1 Skilled Listening
5.2 Social Behavior
6.1 Read and Write Qualitative Scholarly Articles in Psychology
7.2 Evaluate the Quality of Online and Printed Information
8.1 Biological Psychology
8.2 Sensation and Perception
9.1 Developmental Psychology
9.2 Motivation and Emotion
9.3 Personality
9.4 Social Psychology
9.5 Abnormal Psychology

The following writing exercises are new in the third edition:

Read & Write 1.1: Analyze a Chapter from a Psychology Classic
Read & Write 1.2: Critique a Lead News Article
Read & Write 2.1: Identify an Unanswered Question in Psychology
Read & Write 2.2: Write a Chapter Outline
Read & Write 3.2: Proofread the Mental Health Bill

1

READ AND WRITE TO
UNDERSTAND PEOPLE

1.1 READING PSYCHOLOGY ANALYTICALLY

It doesn't matter how good a reader you are right now, how much you enjoy reading, how often you read, what sorts of texts you like and what sorts you avoid, how fast you read, or how effective your level of retention is. The fact is that the remainder of your academic career—the remainder, in fact, of your life—would be made richer if you were better at reading than you are now. This book attempts to make you a better reader, first by offering you tips for improvement—suggestions aimed at enhancing your enjoyment and understanding of any text—and second by supplying you with exercises to improve your reading in the specific discipline of psychology.

But why do we need improvement in reading? It's such a basic skill, something we all learned to do in grade school. Right?

Well, sort of. Our grade school teachers taught us the basics: how to distinguish words in the characters on a page, how to pace ourselves through a sentence or a paragraph to arrive at a coherent meaning. Without these fundamental skills, we couldn't read at all. That's what elementary school focuses on: giving us the basics.

The problem is, there is more to reading than just those first few steps. If there weren't, then we would all be able to read any text pretty much as well as anybody else. It goes without saying, however, that all of us read at different levels of comprehension and different levels of enjoyment, depending on what it is we're reading. We are all different people, each with our own preferences and unique set of experiences that resonate easily to certain stimuli and less easily to others.

Think of all the different worlds you inhabit, your favorite pastimes, hobbies, sports, school subjects. Each is its own world, with its own set of rules and traditions, modes of behavior and thought, and language. Do you remember the first time you watched a college or professional basketball game on television? The action on the court was no doubt dizzying, but so was the conversation by which the sportscasters and commentators explained each play as it happened. What's a "pick and roll"? A "double double"? Or, for that matter, a "triple double"? Why do some penalties allow for a free throw or two while some don't? Basketball is a world with its own rules, its own ways of thinking and speaking. How long did it take you to become comfortable in this world—to become an *insider*?

To read well in virtually any subject, particularly in any school subject or profession, it is essential that you acknowledge to yourself, as you begin to read, that you are entering a new world, one inhabited by insiders and one that can be difficult to understand for people who aren't insiders. For example, if you overhear two psychologists discussing the state of their profession over dinner, you might hear something like this: "Yes, you are right, progress has been made. CBT and ABA initiatives have devised effective BIPs for GAD, ODD, and LDs. But don't forget, many co-morbids, BPDs, codependents, and dissociatives still ask us to check out the *DSM* to verify our duty to warn."

Becoming an insider requires energy and imagination and, above all, a shift in attitude. In the meantime it is still possible for us to learn how to tailor our reading skills to texts in different disciplines, including those for which we do not have a natural affinity or a set of closely related personal experiences.

Whether you are reading a textbook chapter, a newspaper or magazine article, an essay in a journal, a book, or a blog, read on for some tips to help you master the text.

Read with Patience

Different texts require different degrees of patience from the reader. Be sure, when you undertake to read a text written in a discipline with which you have little familiarity, that you are willing to read carefully to allow the material—and the world from which it comes—to sink in. Reading with patience means being willing to perform certain prereading activities that can aid in your mastery of the text. Some of these activities are discussed below.

Reading with patience requires making sure to give yourself plenty of time to read the text. If it's a homework assignment, don't start reading for the first time the night before it's due. The sense of urgency—if not panic—that attends a rushed reading assignment can drive the material right out of your head before you can master it. Reading with patience also means eliminating distractions, such as the television blaring in the next room or a device driving songs through those earbuds you're wearing. Too many people in the apartment? Go find a coffee shop with only a few customers. Hit the library and find a comfortable chair in the reading room. Would a snack help or hurt your ability to immerse yourself in the text?

Reading with patience means arranging your environment to enhance the clarity of your reading experience. The optimal environment is different for different people. But remember, studies continue to demonstrate that multitasking and external activities reduce your reading effectiveness. The point is to do whatever you can do to *reduce your resistance to reading*.

Clarify Your Goals before You Begin to Read

What is it *exactly* that you hope reading this text will do for you? Are you merely looking for a few facts to shore up a point you are making in a paper? Are you cramming for a test? Are you working to establish a general understanding of a particular topic or the contours and details of a many-sided argument? Or are you merely reading to amuse yourself? Whatever the reasons that sent you to the text, remind yourself of them from time to time as you read, comparing what you are finding in the text to whatever it is you are hoping to find. Be ready to revise your goals depending on what you learn from the text. If, for example, you begin reading an article in the *Atlantic* that examines personality changes during adolescence, do you become interested in exploring changes in adolescent culture in the current generation?

Explore the Text's Format

Reconnoiter before Diving In   You need to remember that the writer, whoever it is, wants you to understand his or her writing and has used a variety of devices to help you. If the text has headings and subheadings, read through them first, to see if they give you a sense of the author's direction and purpose. Note any distinctions among the headings, some of which may use larger and/or boldface type to underscore their organizational importance. Understanding the relationship among headings can help you determine the shape of the text's argument.

Are there illustrations? Graphs? Charts? Photographs or drawings? If so, a quick study of them will enhance your understanding of the text's goals and its potential usefulness to you.

Keep in Mind the Writer's Goals

Read carefully the first paragraph or first page of the text, looking for the writer's main idea and strategy for presenting it. Even if you don't find a specific thesis statement—a sentence or two explaining clearly the purpose of the text—most writers will find a way to signal to you what it is they hope their text accomplishes. Sometimes the thesis is in the title, as it is for a July 2016 *New York Times* article by Amanda Taub, with the following title: "A Social Reflex: Police and Blacks, Seeing Threat, Close Ranks." Notice how the title of this article implies a question, namely, *How does violence congeal the unity of social groups and their animosity toward other groups?* The article states that "even if facts show that there is no real danger, 'it's the perception of threat from an out-group, regardless of the actual presence of a threat, that predicts prejudice.' . . . This is driven in part by a phenomenon that psychologists refer to as the 'ultimate attribution error,' in which people attribute another group's positive actions to random chance or circumstance but assume that negative actions reflect the group's core nature."[1]

Remember, too, that there is always another goal the writer hopes to achieve: *to change you.* The writer invites you to step a little farther and to look from a slightly different angle than ever before into the world of the text, whatever that world might be: psychology, cuisine, sports, fashion design, music, animal physiology, higher mathematics, film history, or something else. The text is the writer's way of asking you to pass through a doorway into a possibly unfamiliar environment that, the writer is convinced, offers you a worthwhile experience. As you read and

---

[1]   Taub, A. (2016, July 12). A social reflex: Police and Blacks, seeing threat, close ranks. *New York Times.* Retrieved from https://www.nytimes.com/2016/07/13/us/police-shootings-race.html

understand the text, you are becoming more of an insider in that particular environment, broadening the way you look at the world.

Take Notes

Jot Down Notes Based on Your Early Explorations of Text Features   Your assessment of critical features—headings, illustrations, the introduction—has no doubt set up expectations in your mind about the direction and content of the text. Writing those expectations down quickly, in a list perhaps, and then comparing these notes to what you find as you actually read the text can help bring the material into sharp relief in your mind.

Note-Taking Strategies   Your goal in taking down notes is to help you remember those elements in the text that your reading tells you will be useful to you. Two strategies for effective note-taking stand out:

1. Restating the material from the text in your own words
2. Phrasing notes in a way that establishes a dialogue with the text's writer

Restate Noteworthy Material in Your Own Words   Any method of note-taking that requires you to rewrite the text in your own words requires you to engage the text at its most basic level: that of its language. In order to restate the text, you have to understand it. Merely copying the text's words doesn't require the level of engagement that restating does.

Likewise, merely underlining or highlighting text is usually not a very effective way to "own" what it is saying. It's just too easy. You often find yourself highlighting so many passages that the marking loses its effectiveness. Also, highlighting the text doesn't force you to run the material through your own language-making processes, which means you don't participate in the making of meaning as significantly as you should.

Engage in a Give-and-Take with the Author   In addition to recasting the wording of the text into your own words in your notes, you can enhance your understanding by adopting a note format that actually establishes a dialogue with the author.

Ask Questions   Rather than simply finding equivalents for key words or phrases from the text, you might consider phrasing your note in the form of a question or a criticism aimed at the writer's argument. This sort of give-and-take allows you to clarify and control the range of expectations that occur to you as you read. It's a good way to keep your thinking about the text sharp. For example, after reading the *New York Times* article quoted above, you might write:

"Why are black police officers involved in some apparent crimes involving black civilians?"

"How can ultimate attribution error be dispelled?"

It takes very little time to formulate useful questions about the material in almost any text. Never forget the six basic questions: *Who? What? When? Where? Why? How?*

Practice using these questions in the exploratory stages of your reading until asking them becomes reflexive as you read.

Once you have examined the obvious features of a text and formulated some basic questions, you're ready to read.

Observe How Sentence Structure Aids Understanding

Pay Attention to the Little Words   As we thread our way through the pages of any text, our movement is actually directed by little words, mostly prepositions and conjunctions. These little words don't actually add facts or narrative information but instead act as traffic signals preparing us for a shift in emphasis or direction. Phrases like *furthermore, however, on the contrary*, and *nevertheless* reinforce our interpretation of a preceding passage and prepare us to understand how the next passage will fit along with it.

There are words that *add* the meaning of the coming passage to the last one: *also, and, furthermore, not only . . . but also, too.* And there are phrases that *contrast* the preceding passage with the coming one: *but, despite, however, nevertheless, instead of, rather than, yet.* The phrase *of course* indicates that the next fact follows obviously from the last one, as does the word *obviously.* Words such as *if, provided*, and *unless* indicate that the truth contained in the passage you've just read may be changed by what the next passage adds to the argument.

You know such little words so well that it's easy to overlook their usefulness as markers. Don't. They are extremely important to your reading, shoring up your confidence line by line and preparing your mind for the next passage.

Pay Attention to the Rhythms of the Sentences You Are Reading   Often writers invite you to anticipate the way a sentence moves, perhaps by repeating a word, a phrase, or a syntactical structure, setting up a rhythmic expectation in your mind that, when satisfied, adds greatly to your grasp of the passage's meaning.

In his brief address commemorating the establishment of a military cemetery at the Gettysburg Battlefield, Abraham Lincoln uses the repetition of a syntactical pattern in order to stop the forward motion of his speech, to shift its focus from the audience's participation in the ceremony to the sacrifice that has occasioned the need for the graveyard:

> But in a larger sense we cannot dedicate—we cannot consecrate—we cannot hallow—this ground. The brave men, living and dead, who struggled here, have consecrated it, far above our poor power to add or detract.[2]

As You Read, Be Aware of Other Language Tools

Your writer will employ a range of devices calculated to make you feel comfortable in the world of the text. Look for them and allow them to do their work.

- An *analogy* is a comparison between two things that are similar in some important way. Expect to find your writer composing analogies in which some

---

[2]   Lincoln, A. (n.d.). The Gettysburg address. *Abraham Lincoln Online.* Retrieved from http://www .abrahamlincolnonline.org/lincoln/speeches/gettysburg.htm (Original work published 1863)

element of the world of the text—an element unfamiliar to a noninsider—is compared with some element more common to everyday life.

Here's an example: When Sigmund Freud wanted to explain his three-level conception of how the human brain works, he developed what is now known as his iceberg analogy. The tip of the mind's "iceberg" is normal consciousness. We feel sleepy or become afraid or notice someone's unusual behavior. The next level down is the preconscious, the realm of such practical matters as a need to pick up groceries on the way home or to thank a friend for a favor. We may not be thinking of these things directly at a particular moment, but they hover in waiting nonetheless. The final and most powerful level is the unconscious, an area driven by deep desires that fall below our conscious awareness but that heavily influence our actions.[3]

Analogies can be helpful in explaining human behavior. One effective way to evaluate the accuracy of an observation, for example, is to propose an analogy and then discuss the extent to which it precisely represents the observation in question.

- Psychologists are well aware that *concrete details*—details that evoke and engage the senses—can often do more to communicate meaning and intent than the most elaborate abstract description. A powerful example is the campaign ad that Lyndon Johnson ran, just once, on television in his 1964 presidential race against Republican Senator Barry Goldwater. Instead of offering a spoken appeal for voters to reject what Johnson's campaign was painting as Goldwater's dangerously warlike attitude toward the Soviet Union, the ad simply showed a little girl standing in a field, pulling petals off a flower, and counting them as they fall, until the girl's soft voice is suddenly replaced by a man's, echoing harshly the countdown to a rocket launch, and the image of the girl's face is replaced by the image of an exploding nuclear bomb.[4]

Test Your Recollection

It is easy to forget material right after you've learned it, so as you read you'll need to stop occasionally and say back to yourself the material you have just acquired. Recite it to yourself *in your own words* to make sure you have truly assimilated the content. This recollection is an important part of the reading process, but it can be dangerous in that if you stop to recollect too often, you can lose your sense of forward motion through the text. So, no matter how often you find yourself stopping to recollect material, and it may happen frequently in a difficult text, try never to stop for long. Remember that the very next sentence may unravel the difficulty that has induced you to make a momentary stop. *Keep going.*

---

[3] McLeod, S. (2013). Sigmund Freud. *SimplyPsychology*. Retrieved from http://www.simplypsychology.org/Sigmund-Freud.html

[4] Babb, D. (2014, September 5). LBJ's 1964 attack ad "Daisy" leaves a legacy for modern campaigns. *Washington Post.* Retrieved from https://www.washingtonpost.com/opinions/lbjs-1964-attack-ad-daisy-leaves-a-legacy-for-modern-campaigns/2014/09/05/d00e66b0-33b4-11e4-9e92-0899b306bbea_story.html

Reread

The single most effective strategy for mastering a text is to reread it. The first time through you are finding your way, and the text's concepts, facts, and lines of argument are forming themselves in your mind as you read, which means you have difficulty anticipating the text's direction. To use an analogy, reading a challenging text for the first time is like driving down a twisting country road at night, one you have never traveled before, with only your car's headlights to guide you. But once you've experienced that road, you will be able to navigate it again more confidently, anticipating its tricky turns. The same thing happens when you reread a text. Having been there before, you now know where the argument is going and can see more clearly not only what the writer is trying to say but his or her motives for saying it.

Rereading as an aid to understanding a text is most effective once you have gotten through the *entire* text. Only then will you have experienced the entire shape of the writer's argument and can commit your entire attention to clarifying passages that were difficult during your first run-through.

Pacing Is Vital

How can you possibly pay attention to all the reading tips just discussed and get any sense at all out of the text they are trying to help you understand? Practice. Learning how to improve your reading effectiveness takes time. Try one or two of the suggestions often enough to incorporate them into your reading routine, and then move on to others. The more reading you do, the better you'll get at it, and the wider and more interesting your world will become.

Read & Write 1.1   Analyze a Chapter from a Psychology Classic

In 1890 Harvard University Professor William James (1842–1910), a founding scholar of both psychology and religion, published *The Principles of Psychology*. Your task is to read the introduction to this book, which you will find in your university library or online in pdf format here: https://archive.org/details/theprinciplesofp01jameuoft. Then read it again. Applying the strategies discussed above for enhancing reader involvement, write an essay in which you discuss the similarities and differences between psychology today and the discipline as William James portrayed it in 1890.

1.2   READING NEWS AS INTERPERSONAL INFLUENCE

Psychology: Helping You Perceive and Evaluate Influence in Society

A central focus of psychology is the study of the mechanisms of influence: personal, social, economic, cultural, religious, and political. One of the most important mechanisms of influence on the planet, and an important topic in political and social psychology, is what we commonly call the news. Without a free-flowing supply of news in a country, freedom, democracy, and security are unavailable, and personal vitality and fulfillment for most people are severely impaired. Even with a free flow of news, those who control that flow have enormous influence.

Influence Is Deciding Who Shows Up on the Radar Screen and the Size of Their Blip

Control of the news means controlling what people know and what they don't know. It means controlling who makes the local, national, and international radar screen and who does not. A local news story about a child dying of cancer can produce an immediate inflow of assistance that many other families in similar situations must go without. In some areas of the world, making the radar screen is a matter of life and death for millions of people. At any particular time, tens of thousands of people worldwide face war, disease, famine, and natural disasters. Some get a lot of help, some get moderate assistance, and some get virtually none at all. What determines who gets what?

Politics always plays a role, but publicity can be equally important. "The pen is mightier than the sword," writes Edward Bulwer-Lytton in his play *Richelieu: Or, The Conspiracy* (1839).[5] Following are three historical examples of the power of the press.

To Save Lives One of the most notable and successful efforts to save lives by exploiting the media radar screen was conducted by Mohandas Gandhi (1869–1948). Having developed techniques of nonviolent resistance to racial oppression in South Africa in the 1890s, Gandhi went to India during World War I and began organizing peaceful demonstrations against the British occupation there. His first task was to liberate India from the British without a violent civil war. Through several prison terms, large-scale protest marches, and well-orchestrated trips to London to see top officials, Gandhi attracted press attention wherever he went. When civil war between Hindus and Muslims began to threaten India after World War II, Gandhi walked hundreds of miles through villages of both religions. In so doing, Gandhi not only succeeded in averting a war of independence, saving hundreds of thousands of lives, but also averted a civil war, saving hundreds of thousands more. His deep commitment to justice and nonviolence and his superior management of publicity helped him save more lives than anyone else in history.

To Defeat Racism Sometimes lives are saved when the words and actions of certain people are denied recognition on the media radar screen. Atop Magnetic Mountain, overlooking the rolling verdant hills of Eureka Springs, Arkansas, stands a 65.5-foot-tall statue of Jesus, beckoning visitors to *The Great Passion Play*, a dramatic depiction of the last week of Jesus's life. The play and statue are monuments to the energies of evangelist and political organizer Gerald L. K. Smith (1898–1976). A powerful speaker who attracted sizeable crowds, Smith

---

5   Bulwer-Lytton, E. (186-?). *Richelieu: Or, the conspiracy, a play in five acts*, II, ii, p. 39. In *Making of America*. New York, NY: Samuel French. Ann Arbor, MI: University of Michigan Library (2005). Retrieved from http://name.umdl.umich.edu/AAX3994.0001.001 (Original work published 1839)

was a Christian nationalist and white supremacist. Virulently anti-Semitic, Smith founded the America First Party in 1946. A firm believer that the Jews killed Jesus and that they have been a primary source of evil ever since, after World War II, Smith preached against Jews while defending Nazis at every opportunity. The Holocaust, in which several million Jews were killed in Nazi death camps, was a fresh memory in the late 1940s and early 1950s. The world over, Jews knew they had to energetically combat anti-Semitism wherever they encountered it, so Smith naturally became a prime concern for the Jewish Anti-Defamation League (ADL) and the American Jewish Committee (AJC). Jewish leaders adopted a tactic of "dynamic silence." They asked newspaper editors to first consider the extent to which their coverage was helping Smith draw so much attention. Then they asked the editors to consider whether or not Smith's hatred-filled rants deserved the free publicity they were getting. They proposed that if the papers stopped covering Smith's rallies, his movement would dry up along with his publicity. The editors agreed and stopped coverage, and Smith's momentum declined. Although Smith continued work on his statue and passion play, his movement never recovered.

To Make Policy, Not Always for the Better   Finally, sometimes the radar screen is purposefully distorted in the interest of particular news media. By the late 1880s, Cuba was a prosperous Spanish colony whose sugar sweetened American muffins, piña coladas, and Coca-Colas. But U.S.-owned Hawaiian plantations became sufficiently powerful to gain import tax advantages from Congress. Its main market for its primary product gone, Cuba's economy collapsed. Penniless and hungry, the plantation workers revolted. Spain responded by sending troops, who rounded up thousands of protesters and herded them into *concentrado* camps, a name borrowed by the Nazis for use in the Holocaust. A decade of unrest pursued, turmoil that unfortunately became useful to newspaper czar William Randolph Hearst, who wanted to create news to outsell his competition, and Assistant Secretary of the Navy (later President) Theodore Roosevelt, who wanted to enhance America's image as a world power. Pumping up false charges of cruelty against Spain (in what became known as *yellow journalism*), and blaming Spain for the sinking of the American battleship *Maine* in Havana Harbor, the United States declared war on Spain in 1898 and seized control of Spanish territories in the Caribbean and the Pacific.

Because psychologists spend a lot of their time reading newspapers, it is vital for them to know how to read skillfully—how to understand and evaluate newspaper material accurately and quickly. Learning to do so requires the mastery of certain reading techniques that people may not typically apply to the reading of their local paper. This chapter offers tips that can help you read a newspaper like a psychologist.

Understand the Task

In addition to entertainment and advertising, the content of any newspaper includes news and opinions, and because these two categories can be easily and even intentionally confused, and because accurately differentiating them is essential, let's take a quick look at them.

News is composed of two types of data: information and analysis.

- *Information* is composed of facts, specifically, accounts of events and background. The title of an account of an event could be "Conservative Christians Hold 'City on a Hill' Conference." A background statement could be, "This is the third time this year that Conservative Christians have met in Washington, DC."
- *Analysis* is comprised of interpretations of the information rendered in the news story. Having observed the goings-on at the "City on a Hill" conference, the reporter now interprets what he or she has witnessed there: "A primary purpose of the conference seems to have been to encourage Conservative Christians to develop a new strategy to restrict abortions."

Opinions are evaluations of the information reported in newspapers and are composed of editorials, op-ed pieces (opinion pieces written by named authors who are not on the newspaper's staff), opinion columns, blogs, and other contributions, such as transcripts of interviews. An opinion concerning the "City on a Hill" conference, published in one of the newspaper's editorials, might read, "Once again conservatives seek to consolidate their weakening power by angering a variety of social constituencies." Clearly, the line between analysis and opinion is a thin one.

A Conundrum   On a daily basis, high-quality newspapers like the *New York Times* and the *Wall Street Journal* attempt to clearly identify and separate news from opinion. Their integrity and credibility depend on their success. Their articles are clearly identifiable as news or opinion, and most of the time their news articles have a high degree of objectivity. Opinion is opinion and is persuasive to the extent it seems reasonable or appeals to a certain prejudice. Intelligent readers rarely confuse opinion with news.

But "news" suffers from a congenital defect. No matter how objective a reporter tries to be, perfection is intrinsically beyond reach. Philosopher Karl Popper (1902–1994) was fond of starting courses with a simple command to his students: "Observe." He would stand quietly and wait until a student would break the tension with the question, "Observe what?" "Precisely," would be Popper's retort. His point was that no observation is purely objective and value-free. The moment we try to observe, we necessarily choose what to observe, and that choice is always full of values.

When editors assign stories, their selections are affected not only by their experienced sense of importance but also by their perceptions of the prospective author and by their estimate of what sells well. Therefore, although "objective reporting" is the hallmark of a good newspaper, good reporters understand and exploit the tension between "news" and "opinion," allowing, at least to some extent, their quest for relevance to temper their thirst for facts.

Read the Front Page

Daily newspapers are much like highway maps, providing thousands of bits of information that together form a coherent web that can be imagined as a compact image of life on this planet, or on part of it, on any particular day. The newspaper's front page is the symbol key to that map. Start your newspaper reading by noting both what is included on the front page and what is not. Following is your front-page analytical checklist.

Content   What gets premium front-page coverage tells you what the newspaper's priorities and biases are. Here are stories listed in the front-page section of the *New York Times* online (http://www.nytimes.com) for August 10, 2016:

- Donald Trump Suggests "Second Amendment People" Could Act Against Hillary Clinton
- Donald Trump's Support Among Republican Women Starts to Slide
- Justice Department to Release Blistering Report of Racial Bias by Baltimore Police
- In the Olympic Pool, Contempt for Drug Cheats Rises to the Surface
- Gymnastics Team Final: Simone Biles and the U.S. Women Go for Gold
- Mexico's Richest Man Confronts a New Foe: The State That Helped Make Him Rich
- Minorities Suffer from Unequal Pain Treatment
- Emails Renew Questions About Clinton Foundation and State Dept. Overlap
- Putin and Erdogan Vow to Repair Ties as West Watches Nervously
- "They Will Kill Us": Afghan Translators Plead for Delayed U.S. Visas
- Judge Rejects Rod Blagojevich's Plea for Reduced Sentence
- Justice Department to Streamline Tracking of Police Killings
- Transporting the Dead: A Booming but Lightly Regulated Industry
- Review: Sarasota Ballet Shows Its Mastery of Frederick Ashton's Marvels
- Review: "Troilus and Cressida," a Trojan War Love Story
- M.I.T., N.Y.U. and Yale Are Sued Over Retirement Plan Fees
- Facebook Blocks Ad Blockers, but It Strives to Make Ads More Relevant
- City Kitchen: 3 Quick and Savory Recipes for Peak-of-the-Season Tomatoes

By contrast, here are the articles on the cover of the online *New York Post* (http://www.nypost.com) for the same day, August 10, 2016:

- Julian Assange suggests DNC staffer was shot dead for being a "source"
- ESPN stalwart John Saunders dead at 61
- Malia Obama appears to be smoking pot at Lollapalooza
- Two police officers shot in Arkansas
- These stunning model triplets truly live identical lives
- The GOP majority could get wiped out in November
- WTF is going on with James Franco's hair?

What assumptions about each paper's character can you make by comparing the contents of these front pages?

Layout   Position on the front page reflects the editor's estimate of the importance of an article. A banner headline is big-time news. Newspapers are in the traditional habit of placing the lead article in the upper right corner of the front page, because when they are displayed on old-style newsstands the papers are folded in the middle and arrayed so that the upper right part of the paper is seen by passers-by. The second most important story appears on the upper left. The bigger the title font, the more important the article.

Everything about the front page is done on purpose. Did you ever notice that when you enter Walgreen's to pick up a prescription, the pharmacy is in the rear of the store? Try getting to the pharmacy without being distracted, if ever so slightly, by candy, cosmetics, cuticle clippers, coffee cups, crayons, and birthday cards. The front page of a typical newspaper is organized a bit like the aisles in a Walgreen's, offering something for everyone.

The Structure of an Article   Every article in a newspaper has three jobs to do:

1. Get your attention
2. Tell you the story's bottom line
3. Tell a convincing story in a very short time

These goals require news articles to follow a standard format known as the *inverted pyramid*. While literary stories start with small details and build to a climax at the end, news articles do the opposite. The article title is the "bottom line." It tells you the punchline of the story right up front. Details follow in descending order, the most important ones first. Background and incidentals come last.

Reading News Reports   To accurately read a newspaper article you have a lot of work to do. Happily, as time goes on, you become familiar with the publications, the journalists, their sources, and other matters, but it takes practice. Here is a news article appraisal checklist:

- *Reputation.* What does the reading public think of the newspaper? What does the quality of the front page tell you? Earlier in this chapter you were invited to compare front pages from the *New York Times* and the *New York Post*. Which of these two newspapers would you rather cite as a source for information in your own term paper?
- *Author.* What are the credentials and reputation of the author of the news story? Does he or she have the background to accurately report the news? A newspaper's website normally provides the credentials of its reporters.
- *Information Sources.* What sources of information does the author use? Are they credible? Are they recognized individuals or institutions? Is the information source appropriate for the article's topic? Is the topic timely and the information it provides up to date? Does the author include multiple sources to support his or her statements?
- *Writing Quality.* Is the article well written? Is it clear and cogent? Does it use a lot of jargon? Can you understand it? Does it employ many adverbs? In general, adjectives and adverbs tend to be "opinion words" rather than "news words." Why, for example, is the adverb in the following sentence questionable? "Morgan *willfully* ran over my bicycle in the driveway."
- *Quantity of Information.* Is the article sufficiently comprehensive to substantiate its thesis? Does it answer the essential questions *Who? What? When? Where? Why?* and *How?*

- *Unsupported Assumptions.* Beware statements like this: "Statistics prove that children in traditional two-parent households are happier than children in other households." What statistics? Does the article identify them?
- *Balance.* If you are reading a *news* article about a controversial subject, the article should include information from more than one side of an argument. Also, a well-written *opinion* article will normally identify the content of opposing views, even if only to discredit them.

Read & Write 1.2 Critique a Lead News Article

Read the following article from the *New York Times*, a highly respected newspaper, and examine, in a response of approximately 500 words, the hierarchy of flow within it. Is it an inverted pyramid? Explain.

The New York Times Sunday Review NEWS ANALYSIS

Do Your Friends Actually Like You?

By KATE MURPHY AUG. 6, 2016

THINK of all the people with whom you interact during the course of a day, week, month and year. The many souls with whom you might exchange a greeting or give a warm embrace; engage in chitchat or have a deeper conversation. All those who, by some accident of fate, inhabit your world. And then ask yourself who among them are your friends—your true friends. Recent research indicates that only about half of perceived friendships are mutual. That is, someone you think is your friend might not be so keen on you. Or, vice versa, as when someone you feel you hardly know claims you as a bestie.

It's a startling finding that has prompted much discussion among psychologists, neuroscientists, organizational behavior experts, sociologists and philosophers. Some blame human beings' basic optimism, if not egocentrism, for the disconnect between perceived and actual friendships. Others point to a misunderstanding of the very notion of friendship in an age when "friend" is used as a verb, and social inclusion and exclusion are as easy as a swipe or a tap on a smartphone screen. It's a concern because the authenticity of one's relationships has an enormous impact on one's health and well-being.

"People don't like to hear that the people they think of as friends don't name them as friends," said Alex Pentland, a computational social science researcher at M.I.T. and co-author of a recent study published in the journal PLOS One titled "Are You Your Friends' Friend? Poor Perception of Friendship Ties Limits the Ability to Promote Behavioral Change."

The study analyzed friendship ties among 84 subjects (ages 23 to 38) in a business management class by asking them to rank one another on a five-point continuum of closeness from "I don't know this person" to "One of my best friends." The feelings were mutual 53 percent of the time while the expectation of reciprocity was pegged at 94 percent. This is consistent with data from several other friendship studies conducted over the past decade, encompassing more than 92,000 subjects, in which the reciprocity rates ranged from 34 percent to 53 percent.

Mr. Pentland said it could be that "the possibility of nonreciprocal friendship challenges one's self-image." But the problem may have more to do with confusion over what friendship is. Ask people to define friendship—even researchers like Mr. Pentland who study it—and you'll get an uncomfortable silence followed by "er" or "um."

"Friendship is difficult to describe," said Alexander Nehamas, a professor of philosophy at Princeton, who in his latest book, "On Friendship," spends almost 300 pages trying to do just that. "It's easier to say what friendship is not and, foremost, it is not instrumental."

It is not a means to obtain higher status, wangle an invitation to someone's vacation home or simply escape your own boredom. Rather, Mr. Nehamas said, friendship is more like beauty or art, which kindles something deep within us and is "appreciated for its own sake."

Yet one of the most recognized treatises on friendship is Dale Carnegie's decidedly instrumental "How to Win Friends and Influence People." Pop stars like Taylor Swift and Drake are admired for their strategic, if not propagandist, friendships. And, of course, social media sites are platforms for showcasing friendships to enhance personal image.

"Treating friends like investments or commodities is anathema to the whole idea of friendship," said Ronald Sharp, a professor of English at Vassar College, who teaches a course on the literature of friendship. "It's not about what someone can do for you, it's who and what the two of you become in each other's presence."

He recalled the many hours he spent in engrossing conversation with his friend Eudora Welty, who was known not only for her Pulitzer Prize-winning fiction but also for her capacity for friendship. Together they edited "The Norton Book of Friendship," an anthology of works on the topic. "The notion of doing nothing but spending time in each other's company has, in a way, become a lost art," replaced by volleys of texts and tweets, Mr. Sharp said. "People are so eager to maximize efficiency of relationships that they have lost touch with what it is to be a friend."

By his definition, friends are people you take the time to understand and allow to understand you.

Because time is limited, so, too, is the number of friends you can have, according to the work of the British evolutionary psychologist Robin I.M. Dunbar. He describes layers of friendship, where the topmost layer consists of only one or two people, say a spouse and best friend with whom you are most intimate and interact daily. The next layer can accommodate at most four people for whom you have great affinity, affection and concern and who require weekly attention to maintain. Out from there, the tiers contain more casual friends with whom you invest less time and tend to have a less profound and more tenuous connection. Without consistent contact, they easily fall into the realm of acquaintance. You may be friendly with them but they aren't friends.

"There is a limited amount of time and emotional capital we can distribute, so we only have five slots for the most intense type of relationship," Mr. Dunbar said. "People may say they have more than five but you can be pretty sure they are not high-quality friendships."

Such boasting implies they have soul mates to spare in a culture where we are taught that leaning on someone is a sign of weakness and power is not letting others affect you. But friendship requires the vulnerability of caring as well as revealing things about yourself that don't match the polished image in your Facebook profile or Instagram feed, said Mr. Nehamas at Princeton. Trusting that your bond will continue, and might even be strengthened, despite your shortcomings and inevitable misfortunes, he said, is a risk many aren't willing to take.[6]

[6]   Murphy, K. (2016, August 6). Do your friends actually like you? *New York Times*. Retrieved from http://nyti .ms/2aWZCjy

2

READ AND WRITE

EFFECTIVELY

Writing is a way of ordering your experience. Think about it. No matter what you are writing—it may be a paper for your Introduction to Psychology class, a tweet, a Facebook post, a grocery list—you are putting pieces of your world together in new ways and making yourself freshly conscious of those pieces. This is one of the reasons why writing is so hard. From the infinite welter of data that your mind continually processes and locks in your memory, you are selecting only certain items significant to the task at hand, relating them to other items, and phrasing them with a new coherence. You are mapping a part of your universe that has hitherto been unknown territory. You are gaining a little more control over the processes by which you interact with the world around you.

This is why the act of writing, no matter what its result, is never insignificant. It is always *communication*—if not with another human being, then with yourself. It is a way of making a fresh connection with your world.

Writing therefore is also one of the best ways to learn. This statement may sound odd at first. If you are an unpracticed writer, you may share a common notion that the only purpose of writing is to express what you already know or think. According to this view, any learning that you as a writer might have experienced has already occurred by the time your pen meets the paper; your task is thus to inform and even surprise the reader. But, if you are a practiced writer, you know that at any moment as you write, you are capable of surprising yourself. And it is that surprise that you look for: the shock of seeing what happens in your own mind when you drop an old, established opinion into a batch of new facts or bump into a cherished belief from a different angle. Writing synthesizes new understanding for the writer. E. M. Forster's famous question, "How do I know what I think until I see what I say?"[1] is one that all of us could ask. We make meaning as we write, jolting ourselves into a larger and more interesting universe by way of little, surprising discoveries.

---

[1] Forster, E. M. (1956). *Aspects of the novel* (p. 101). New York, NY: Harvest. (Original work published 1927)

A Simultaneous Tangle of Activities

One reason that writing is difficult is that it is not actually a single activity at all but a process consisting of several activities that can overlap, with two or more sometimes operating simultaneously as you labor to organize and phrase your thoughts. (We will discuss these activities later in this chapter.) The writing process, an often frustrating search for meaning and for the best way to articulate that meaning, tends to be sloppy for everyone.

Frustrating though that search may sometimes be, it need not be futile. Remember this: the writing process uses skills that we all have. The ability to write is not some magical competence bestowed on the rare, fortunate individual. We are all capable of phrasing thoughts clearly and in a well-organized fashion. But learning how to do so takes practice.

The one sure way to improve your writing is to write.

One of the toughest but most important jobs in writing is to maintain enthusiasm for your writing project. Such commitment may sometimes be hard to achieve, given the difficulties that are inherent in the writing process and that can worsen when the project is unappealing at first glance. How, for example, can you be enthusiastic about having to write a paper describing the play activities of children, when you have never once thought about child play and can see no use in doing so now?

Sometimes unpracticed student writers fail to assume responsibility for keeping themselves interested in their writing. No matter how hard it may seem at first to drum up interest in your topic, you have to do it—that is, if you want to write a paper you can be proud of, one that contributes useful material and a fresh point of view to the topic. One thing is guaranteed: if you are bored with your writing, your reader will be, too. So what can you do to keep your interest and energy level high?

Challenge yourself. Think of the paper not as an assignment but as a piece of writing that has a point to make. To get this point across persuasively is the real reason you are writing, not because a teacher has assigned you a project. If someone were to ask you why you are writing your paper and your immediate, unthinking response is, "Because I've been given a writing assignment" or "Because I want a good grade" or some other nonanswer along these lines, your paper may be in trouble.

If, on the other hand, your first impulse is to explain the challenge of your main point—"I'm writing to describe the influence of sleep patterns on children's play activities"—then you are thinking usefully about your topic.

Maintain Self-Confidence

Having confidence in your ability to write well about your topic is essential for good writing. This does not mean that you will always know what the result of a particular writing activity will be. In fact, you have to cultivate your ability to tolerate a high degree of uncertainty while weighing evidence, testing hypotheses, and experimenting with organizational strategies and wording. Be ready for temporary confusion and for seeming dead ends, and remember that every writer faces these obstacles. It is out of your struggle to combine fact with fact, to buttress conjecture with evidence, that order will arise.

Do not be intimidated by the amount and quality of work that others have already done in your field of inquiry. The array of opinion and evidence that confronts you in the literature can be confusing. But remember that no important topic is ever exhausted. There are always gaps—questions that have not been satisfactorily explored in either the published research or the prevailing popular opinion. It is in these gaps that you establish your own authority, your own sense of control.

Remember that the various stages of the writing process reinforce each other. Establishing a solid motivation strengthens your sense of confidence about the project, which in turn influences how successfully you organize and write. If you start out well, use good work habits, and allow ample time for the various activities to coalesce, you should produce a paper that will reflect your best work, one that your audience will find both readable and useful.

2.1   GET INTO THE FLOW OF WRITING

The Nature of the Process

As you engage in the writing process, you are doing many things at once. While planning, you are, no doubt, defining the audience for your paper at the same time that you are thinking about its purpose. As you draft the paper, you may organize your next sentence while revising the one you have just written. Different parts of the writing process overlap, and much of the difficulty of writing occurs because so many things happen at once. Through practice—in other words, through *writing*—it is possible to learn to control those parts of the process that can in fact be controlled and to encourage those mysterious, less controllable activities.

No two people go about writing in exactly the same way. It is important to recognize the routines—modes of thought as well as individual exercises—that help you negotiate the process successfully. It is also important to give yourself as much time as possible to complete the process. Procrastination is one of the writer's greatest enemies. It saps confidence, undermines energy, and destroys concentration. Writing regularly and following a well-planned schedule as closely as possible often make the difference between a successful paper and an embarrassment.

Although the various parts of the writing process are interwoven, there is naturally a general order in the work of writing. You have to start somewhere! What follows is a description of the various stages of the writing process—planning, drafting, revising, editing, and proofreading—along with suggestions on how to approach each most successfully.

Plan   Planning includes all activities that lead to the writing of the first draft of a paper. The particular activities in this stage differ from person to person. Some writers, for instance, prefer to compile a formal outline before writing the draft. Others perform brief writing exercises to jump-start their imaginations. Some draw diagrams; some doodle. Later, we will look at a few starting strategies, and you can determine which may help you.

Now, however, let us discuss certain early choices that all writers must make during the planning stage. These choices concern *topic*, *purpose*, and *audience*, elements that make up the writing context, or the terms under which we all write. Every time you write, even if you are only writing a diary entry or a note to your lab partner, these elements are present. You may not give conscious consideration to all of them in each piece of writing that you do, but it is extremely important to think carefully about them when writing a psychology paper. Some or all of these defining elements may be dictated by your assignment, yet you will always have a degree of control over them.

Select a Topic   No matter how restrictive an assignment may seem, there is no reason to feel trapped by it. Within any assigned subject you can find a range of topics to explore. What you are looking for is a topic that engages your own interest. Let your curiosity be your guide. If, for example, you have been assigned in your Introduction to Psychology class to write about the Muller-Lyer Illusion, then guide yourself to find some issues concerning the topic that interest you. (For example, who came up with this ingenious little perceptual test and when and why? Do different populations respond to the test in different ways? Is age a factor in response? Gender? Geographical location? Political affiliation?) Any good topic comes with a set of questions; you may well find that your interest increases if you simply begin asking questions. One strong recommendation: ask your questions. Like most mental activities, the process of exploring your way through a topic is transformed when you write down your thoughts as they come, instead of letting them fly through your mind unrecorded. Remember the words of Louis Agassiz: "A pen is often the best of eyes."[2]

Although it is vital to be interested in your topic, you do not have to know much about it at the outset of your investigation. In fact, having too heartfelt a commitment to a topic can be an impediment to writing about it; emotions can get in the way of objectivity. It is often better to choose a topic that has piqued your interest yet remained something of a mystery to you—a topic discussed in one of your classes, perhaps, or mentioned on television or in a conversation with friends.

Narrow the Topic   The task of narrowing your topic offers you a tremendous opportunity to establish a measure of control over the writing project. It is up to you to hone your topic to just the right shape and size to suit both your own interests and the requirements of the assignment. Do a good job of it, and you will go a long way toward guaranteeing yourself sufficient motivation and confidence for the tasks ahead. However, if you do not do it well, somewhere along the way you may find yourself directionless and out of energy.

Generally, the first topics that come to your mind will be too large for you to handle in your research paper. For example, the subject of a national mental health policy has recently generated a tremendous number of news reports. Yet despite all the attention, there is still plenty of room for you to investigate the topic on a level that has real meaning for you and that does not merely recapitulate the published research. What about an analysis of how one of the proposed treatment strategies might affect insurance costs for a locally owned business that employs 10 or 20 full-time workers?

The problem with most topics is not that they are too narrow or have been too completely explored but, rather, that they are so rich that it is often difficult to choose the most useful way to address them. Take some time to narrow your topic.

---

[2]   Pearce, C. O. (1958). *A scientist of two worlds: Louis Agassiz* (p. 106). Philadelphia, PA: Lippincott.

Think through the possibilities that occur to you and, as always, jot down your thoughts.

Students in an undergraduate psychology course were told to write an essay of 2,500 words on one of the issues shown below. Next to each general topic is an example of how students narrowed it into a manageable paper topic.

General Topic	Narrowed Topic
Freud	Freud's interpretation of dreams
The human brain	How the structure of the brain shapes personality
The psychology of religion	The psychology of religious conversions
Music	The psychology of repetition

EXERCISE

Without doing research, see how you can narrow the general topics shown below:

Example

General topic	Mental illness
Narrowed topics	The evolution of the concept of mental illness
	Current patterns of mental illness in the United States
	Attitudes toward common types of mental illness

General Topics

Education and child development	Emotional intelligence	Personality types
Social movements	Gender	Criminal behavior
Cognition	Behavior modification	Family systems
Effective management	Learning	Motivation

Once you have selected a narrowed topic, you are ready to make your first foray into research, and you will make at least several more as your project proceeds. Remind yourself of your goal. Unlike fiction or reflective essays, your goal is neither amusement nor self-understanding. Keep in mind that a substantial portion of your college education is to prepare you for a profession and the advanced degrees and scholarship that professions require. Psychology is a social science, with an emphasis on *science*. All science is devoted to a single cause: identifying something that needs to be known and contributing something to knowing it. The purpose of your venture, therefore, is finding something unknown that is worth knowing. Your goal is not to come up with an original idea, although that may happen. Your goal in writing a psychology paper is to begin the task of psychology: find a knowledge gap and fill it. In simple terms, you have two choices:

OPTION 1. Select a topic and find out what is known about it and what remains to be known (see sections 6.2 and 6.4, "Write a Literature Review," of this manual), or

OPTION 2. Select a topic and find out what is known about it and what remains to be known, and conduct research to make a contribution to that knowledge (see chapter 7 for tips on how to conduct research).

Don't Fear Finding the Gap!

Finding a knowledge gap in psychology is easy. Authors of scholarly articles regularly serve them to you at the ends of their articles. For example, in the abstract of an article published in the journal *Psychology of Music*, Dave Miranda, Camille Blais-Rochette, Karole Vaugon, Muna Osman, and Melisa Arias-Valenzuela (2015) explain what their research is about:

> Music is a fundamental cultural product with which adolescents are finely attuned within and across sociocultural contexts. However, very little is known about the intricate interplay among music, psychology, and culture in adolescence. The purpose of this literature review is twofold: (1) to define, ground, and situate a new perspective towards a cultural developmental psychology of music in adolescence; and (2) to find and organize the extant literature pertaining to the cultural and developmental roles of music in adolescence.[3]

If you proceed to the end of their article you will find a section titled "Research Directions," in which the authors identify, in an essay of 770 words, five areas of inquiry that have gaps in knowledge that need to be filled. As you peruse articles under topics of your choice, you will find many gaps waiting to be filled.

But wait! Let's suppose that these University of Ottawa scholars have piqued your interest in their research. At the beginning of the article you will find information on how to contact the first author:

> Dave Miranda, School of Psychology, Faculty of Social Sciences, University of Ottawa, 136 Jean-Jacques Lussier (Vanier Hall), K1N 6N5, Ottawa, ON, Canada. Email: dave.miranda@uottawa.ca

Here is an opportunity to email the lead author with questions or suggestions for your own research project. Most scholars will be glad to share some thoughts to get you started.

Read & Write 2.1 Identify an Unanswered Question in Psychology

Your task here is OPTION 1 above. Select six recent scholarly articles in a subfield of psychology of your choice. Most articles will identify at least one question its authors admit is

---

[3] Miranda, D., Blais-Rochette, C., Vaugon, K., Osman, M., & Arias-Valenzuela, M. (2015). Towards a cultural-developmental psychology of music in adolescence (p. 197). *Psychology of Music, 43*(2), 197–218. Retrieved from http://journals.sagepub.com/doi/full/10.1177/0305735613500700

still unanswered by psychologists. Write a series of six paragraphs, one for each article. Each paragraph will include the following:

- A citation: author, title, publication, date, pages, etc.
- A short paraphrased summary of the abstract of the article
- A statement of at least one thing the authors discovered by conducting their research
- A statement of one thing authors still do not know that would contribute to our knowledge of the topic the authors have researched

2.2 ORGANIZE YOUR QUALITATIVE WRITING

The structure of any particular type of a qualitative psychology paper is governed by a formal pattern. When rigid external controls are placed on their writing, some writers feel that their creativity is hampered by a kind of paint-by-numbers approach to structure. It is vital to the success of your paper that you never allow yourself to be overwhelmed by the pattern rules for any type of paper. Remember that such controls exist not to limit your creativity but to make the paper immediately and easily useful to its intended audience. It is as necessary to write clearly and confidently in a position paper or a policy analysis paper as in a term paper for English literature, a résumé, a short story, or a job application letter.

A paper that contains all the necessary facts but presents them in an ineffective order will confuse rather than inform or persuade. Although there are various methods of grouping ideas, none is potentially more effective than outlining. Unfortunately, no organizing process is more often misunderstood.

The Importance of Outlining

Outline for Yourself   Outlining can do two jobs. First, it can force you, the writer, to gain a better understanding of your ideas by arranging them according to their interrelationships. There is one primary rule of outlining: ideas of equal weight are placed on the same level within the outline. This rule requires you to determine the relative importance of your ideas. You have to decide which ideas are of the same type or order, and into which subtopic each idea best fits.

If, in the planning stage, you carefully arrange your ideas in a coherent outline, your grasp of your topic will be greatly enhanced. You will have linked your ideas logically together and given a basic structure to the body of the paper. This sort of subordinating and coordinating activity is difficult, however, and as a result, inexperienced writers sometimes begin to write their first draft without an effective outline, hoping for the best. This hope is usually unfulfilled, especially in complex papers involving research.

EXERCISE Organizing Thoughts

Marsden, a student in a class in motivation and emotion, researched the satisfaction that people gain from accomplishing a goal, and he developed a number of statements about his findings. Number them in logical order:

_____ The amount of satisfaction is positively correlated to the importance of the goal.

_____ There are several sources of satisfaction for achieving goals.

_____ The amount of satisfaction is positively correlated to the difficulty of reaching the goal.

_____ The social desirability of reaching a goal is less important than recognition for achieving the goal.

_____ The amount of satisfaction is positively correlated to recognition for achieving the goal.

_____ The amount of satisfaction is positively correlated to the social desirability of reaching the goal.

Outline for Your Reader   The second job an outline can perform is to serve as a reader's blueprint to the paper, summarizing its points and their interrelationships. By consulting your outline, a busy professor can quickly get a sense of your paper's goal and the argument you have used to promote it. The clarity and coherence of the outline help determine how much attention your audience will give to your ideas.

As psychology students, you will be given a great deal of help with the arrangement of your material into an outline to accompany your paper. A look at the formats presented in chapter 3 of this manual will show you how strictly these formal outlines are structured. But, although you must pay close attention to these requirements, do not forget how powerful a tool an outline can be in the early planning stages of your paper.

The Formal Outline Pattern   Following this pattern accurately during the planning stage of your paper helps to guarantee that your ideas are placed logically:

Thesis sentence (precedes the formal outline)

   I. First main idea
      A. First subordinate idea
         1. Reason, example, or illustration
            a. Supporting detail
            b. Supporting detail
            c. Supporting detail
         2. Reason, example, or illustration
            a. Supporting detail
            b. Supporting detail
            c. Supporting detail
      B. Second subordinate idea
  II. Second main idea

Notice that each level of the paper must have more than one entry; for every A there must be at least a B (and, if required, a C, a D, and so on), and for every 1 there must be a 2. This arrangement forces you to _compare ideas_, looking carefully at each one to determine its place among the others. The insistence on assigning relative values to your ideas is what makes an outline an effective organizing tool.

Read&Write 2.2 **Write a Chapter Outline**

At your college library, select a book on a psychology topic of your choice. Select one written by an authority on the subject, someone with strong credentials with respect to the subject matter at hand. Select a chapter in the book and write an outline following the structure above.

2.3 DRAFT, REVISE, EDIT, AND PROOFREAD

Write the Rough Draft

After planning comes the writing of the first draft. Using your thesis and outline as direction markers, you must now weave your amalgam of ideas, data, and persuasion strategies into logically ordered sentences and paragraphs. Although adequate prewriting may facilitate drafting, it still will not be easy. Writers establish their own individual methods of encouraging themselves to forge ahead with the draft, but here are some tips:

- Remember that this is a rough draft, not the final paper. At this stage, it is not necessary that every word be the best possible choice. Do not put that sort of pressure on yourself. You must not allow anything to slow you down now. Writing is not like sculpting in stone, where every chip is permanent; you can always go back to your draft and add, delete, reword, and rearrange. *No matter how much effort you have put into planning, you cannot be sure how much of this first draft you will eventually keep.* It may take several drafts to get one that you find satisfactory.

- Give yourself sufficient time to write. Do not delay the first draft by telling yourself there is still more research to do. You cannot uncover all the material there is to know on a particular subject, so do not fool yourself into trying. Remember that writing is a process of discovery. You may have to begin writing before you can see exactly what sort of research you need to do. Keep in mind that there are other tasks waiting for you after the first draft is finished, so allow for them as you determine your writing schedule.

    More importantly, give yourself time to write because the more time that passes after you have written a draft, the better your ability to view it with objectivity. It is very difficult to evaluate your writing accurately soon after you complete it. You need to cool down, to recover from the effort of putting all those words together. The "colder" you get on your writing, the better you are able to read it as if it were written by someone else and thus acknowledge the changes you will need to make to strengthen the paper.

- Stay sharp. Keep in mind the plan you created as you narrowed your topic, composed a thesis sentence, and outlined the material. But if you begin to feel a strong need to change the plan a bit, do not be afraid to do so. Be ready for surprises dealt you by your own growing understanding of your topic. Your goal is to record your best thinking on the subject as accurately as possible.

Paragraph Development   There is no absolute requirement for the structure of any paragraph in your paper except that all its sentences must be clearly related to each other and each must carry the job of saying what you want to say about your thesis *one step farther*. In other words, any sentence that simply restates something said in another sentence anywhere else in the paper is a waste of your time and the reader's. It isn't unusual for a paragraph to have, somewhere in it, a *topic* sentence that serves as the key to the paragraph's organization and announces the paragraph's connection to the paper's thesis. But not all paragraphs need topic sentences.

What all paragraphs in the paper *do* need is an organizational strategy. Here are four typical organizational models, any one of which, if you keep it in mind, can help you build a coherent paragraph:

- *Chronological organization*: The sentences of the paragraph describe a series of events or steps or observations as they occur over time. This happens, then that, and then that.
- *Spatial organization*: The sentences of the paragraph record details of its subject in some logical order: top to bottom, up to down, outside to inside.
- *General-to-specific organization*: The paragraph starts with a statement of its main idea and then goes into detail as it discusses that idea.
- *Specific-to-general organization*: The paragraph begins with smaller, nuts-and-bolts details, arranging them into a larger pattern that, by the end of the paragraph, leads to the conclusion that is the paragraph's main idea.

These aren't the only organizational strategies available to you, and, of course, different paragraphs in a paper can use different strategies, though a single paragraph that employs more than one organizational plan is risking incoherence. The essential thing to remember is that each sentence in the paragraph must bear a logical relationship to the one before it and the one after it. It is this notion of *interconnectedness* that can prevent you from getting off track and stuffing extraneous material in your paragraphs.

Like all other aspects of the writing process, paragraph development is a challenge. But remember, one of the helpful facts about paragraphs is that they are relatively small, especially compared to the overall scope of your paper. Each paragraph can basically do only one job—handle or help handle a single idea, which is itself only a part of the overall development of the larger thesis idea. That paragraphs are small and aimed at a single task means that revising them is relatively easy. By focusing clearly on the single job a paragraph does and filtering out all the paper's other claims for your attention, you should gain enough clarity of vision during the revision process to understand what you need to do to make that paragraph work better.

Authority   To be convincing, your writing has to be authoritative—that is, you have to sound as if you have complete confidence in your ability to convey your ideas in words. Sentences that sound stilted or that suffer from weak phrasing or the use of clichés are not going to win supporters for the positions that you express in your paper. So a major question becomes, *How can I sound confident?*

Consider these points as you work to convey to your reader that necessary sense of authority:

Level of Formality Tone is one of the primary methods by which you signal to the readers who you are and what your attitude is toward them and toward your topic. Your major decision is which level of language formality is most appropriate to your audience. The informal tone you would use in a letter to a friend might well be out of place in a paper titled "Stress and Mental Health," written for your psychology professor. Remember that tone is only part of the overall decision that you make about how to present your information. Formality is, to some extent, a function of individual word choices and phrasing. For example, is it appropriate to use contractions such as *isn't* or *they'll?* Would the strategic use of a sentence fragment for effect be out of place? The use of informal language, the personal *I*, and the second-person *you* are traditionally forbidden—for better or worse—in certain kinds of writing. Often, part of the challenge of writing a formal paper is simply how to give your prose impact while staying within the conventions.

Jargon One way to lose readers quickly is to overwhelm them with *jargon*— phrases that have a special, usually technical meaning within your discipline but that are unfamiliar to the average reader. The very occasional use of jargon may add an effective touch of atmosphere, but anything more than that will severely dampen a reader's enthusiasm for the paper. Often the writer uses jargon in an effort to impress the reader by sounding lofty or knowledgeable. Unfortunately, the only thing jargon usually does is cause confusion. In fact, the use of jargon indicates a writer's lack of connection to the audience.

Psychological writing is a haven for jargon. Perhaps writers of academic articles believe their readers are all completely attuned to their terminology. Or some may hope to obscure damaging information or potentially unpopular ideas in confusing language. In other cases, the problem could simply be unclear thinking by the writer. Whatever the reason, the fact is that psychology papers too often sound like prose made by machines to be read by machines.

Some students may feel that, to be accepted as psychologists, their papers should conform to the practices of their published peers. This is a mistake. Remember that it is never better to write a cluttered or confusing sentence than a clear one, and burying your ideas in jargon defeats the effort that you went through to form them.

EXERCISE Revising Jargon

What words in the following sentences, from an article in a psychology journal, are jargon? How can you clarify their meaning?

> We calculated the WHR of the face configurations each participant made by dividing the interpupillary distance (x-coordinate right eye-x-coordinate left eye) by the eye-to-mouth height (y-coordinate mouth center-average eye e-coordinate). . . . Figure 3 displays average WHRs (collapsed across particular confederate and outcome) as a function of confederate and game types.[4]

---

[4] Balas, B., & Thomas, L. (2015). Competition makes observers remember faces as more aggressive (p. 712). *Journal of Experimental Psychology, 144*(4), 711–716. Retrieved from doi:10.1037/xge0000078

Actually, if you read the entire article from which this fragment is taken, you will find that the authors have defined the technical terms used here during the course of the article. Not all authors, however, provide the reader this courtesy.

Clichés In the heat of composition, as you are looking for words to help you form your ideas, it is sometimes easy to plug in a *cliché*—a phrase that has attained universal recognition by overuse.

> **Note:** Clichés differ from jargon in that clichés are part of the general public's everyday language, whereas jargon is specific to the language of experts in a field.

Our vocabularies are brimming with clichés:

It's raining cats and dogs.

That issue is as dead as a doornail.

It's time for the governor to face the music.

Angry voters made a beeline for the ballot box.

The problem with clichés is that they are virtually meaningless. Once colorful means of expression, they have lost their color through overuse, and they tend to bleed energy and color from the surrounding words. When revising, replace clichés with fresh wording that more accurately conveys your point.

Descriptive Language Language that appeals to readers' senses will always engage their interest more fully than language that is abstract. This is especially important for writing in disciplines that tend to deal in abstracts, such as psychology. The typical psychology paper, with its discussions of attitudes and behaviors, is often in danger of floating off into abstraction, with each paragraph drifting farther away from the felt life of the readers. Whenever appropriate, appeal to your readers' sense of sight, hearing, taste, touch, or smell.

EXERCISE Using Descriptive Language

Which of these two sentences is more effective?

1. Blanchard's self-esteem had deteriorated badly since her previous therapy session.
2. Blanchard's self-esteem had deteriorated badly since her previous therapy session; her lowered gaze, self-effacing comments, and withdrawn posture had intensified.

Bias-Free and Gender-Neutral Writing Language can be a very powerful method of either reinforcing or destroying cultural stereotypes. By treating the sexes in subtly different ways in your language, you may unknowingly be committing an act of discrimination. A common example is the use of the pronoun *he* to refer to a person whose gender has not been identified.

Some writers, faced with this dilemma, alternate the use of male and female personal pronouns; others use the plural to avoid the need to use a pronoun of either gender:

Sexist: A psychologist should always treat his client with respect.

Corrected: A psychologist should always treat his or her client with respect.

Or: Psychologists should always treat their clients with respect.

Sexist: Man is a political animal.

Corrected: People are political animals.

Remember that language is more than the mere vehicle of your thoughts. Your words shape perceptions for your readers. How well you say something will profoundly affect your readers' response to what you say. Sexist language denies to a large number of your readers the basic right to fair and equal treatment. Make sure your writing is not guilty of this form of discrimination.

Revise

After all the work you have gone through writing it, you may feel "married" to the first draft of your paper. However, revision is one of the most important steps in ensuring your paper's success. Although unpracticed writers often think of revision as little more than making sure all the *i*'s are dotted and *t*'s are crossed, it is much more than that. Revising is *reseeing* the essay, looking at it from other perspectives, trying always to align your view with the one that will be held by your audience. Research indicates that we are actually revising all the time, in every phase of the writing process, as we reread phrases, rethink the placement of an item in an outline, or test a new topic sentence for a paragraph. Subjecting your entire hard-fought draft to cold, objective scrutiny is one of the toughest activities to master, but it is absolutely necessary. You have to make sure that you have said everything that needs to be said clearly and logically. One confusing passage will deflect the reader's attention from where you want it to be. Suddenly the reader has to become a detective, trying to figure out why you wrote what you did and what you meant by it. You do not want to throw such obstacles in the path of understanding.

Here are some tips to help you with revision:

1. Give yourself adequate time for revision. As discussed above, you need time to become "cold" on your paper in order to analyze it objectively. After you have written your draft, spend some time away from it. Then try to reread it as if someone else had written it.

2. Read the paper carefully. This is tougher than it sounds. One good strategy is to read it aloud yourself or to have a friend read it aloud while you listen. (Note, however, that while friends can be fine out-loud readers of your draft, they are usually not the best critics. They are rarely trained in revision techniques and are often unwilling to risk disappointing you by giving your paper a really thorough examination.)

3. Have a list of specific items to check. It is important to revise in an orderly fashion, in stages, first looking at large concerns, such as the overall organization, and then at smaller elements, such as paragraph or sentence structure.

4. Check for unity—the clear and logical relation of all parts of the essay to its thesis. Make sure that every paragraph relates well to the whole of the paper and is in the right place.

5. Check for coherence. Make sure there are no gaps between the various parts of the argument. Look to see that you have adequate transitions everywhere they are needed. *Transitional elements* are markers indicating places where the paper's focus or attitude changes. Such elements can take the form of one word—*however, although, unfortunately, luckily*—or an entire sentence or a paragraph: *In order to fully appreciate the importance of therapy as a concomitant treatment to antidepressants, it is necessary to examine recent studies of the effectiveness of combined treatments.*

   Transitional elements rarely introduce new material. Instead, they are direction pointers, either indicating a shift to new subject matter or signaling how the writer wishes certain material to be interpreted by the reader. Because you, the writer, already know where and why your paper changes direction and how you want particular passages to be received, it can be very difficult for you to catch those places where transition is needed.

6. Avoid unnecessary repetition. Two types of repetition can annoy a reader: repetition of content and repetition of wording.

   Repetition of content occurs when you return to a subject you have already discussed. Ideally, you should deal with a topic once, memorably, and then move on to your next subject. Organizing a paper is a difficult task, however, which usually occurs through a process of enlightenment in terms of purposes and strategies, and repetition of content can happen even if you have used prewriting strategies. What is worse, it can be difficult for you to be aware of the repetition in your own writing. As you write and revise, remember that any unnecessary repetition of content in your final draft is potentially annoying to your readers, who are working to make sense of the argument they are reading and do not want to be distracted by a passage repeating material they have already encountered. You must train yourself, through practice, to look for material that you have repeated unnecessarily.

   Repetition of wording occurs when you overuse certain phrases or words. This can make your prose sound choppy and uninspired, as the following examples demonstrate:

   > The subcommittee's report on ADD treatment reform will surprise a number of people. A number of people will want copies of the report.

   > The chairman said in the weekly meeting that he is happy with the report. He will circulate it to the staff in the morning. He will also make sure that the superintendent has copies.

   > I became upset when I heard how the committee had voted. I called the chairman and expressed my reservations about the committee's decision. I told him I felt that he had let the high school guidance counselors of the state down. I also issued a press statement.

The last passage illustrates a condition known by composition teachers as the *I-syndrome*. Can you hear how such duplicated phrasing can hurt a paper? Your language should sound fresh and energetic. Make sure, before you submit your final draft, to read through your paper carefully, looking for such repetition.

However, not all repetition is bad. You may wish to repeat a phrase for rhetorical effect or special emphasis: *I came. I saw. I conquered.* Just make sure that any repetition in your paper is intentional, placed there to produce a specific effect.

Edit

Editing is sometimes confused with the more involved process of revising. But editing is done later in the writing process, after you have wrestled through your first draft—and maybe your second and third—and arrived at the final draft. Even though your draft now contains all the information you want to impart and has the information arranged to your satisfaction, there are still many factors to check, such as sentence structure, spelling, and punctuation.

It is at this point that an unpracticed writer might be less than vigilant. After all, most of the work on the paper is finished, as the "big jobs" of discovering, organizing, and drafting information have been completed. But watch out! Editing is as important as any other part of the writing process. Any error that you allow in the final draft will count against you in the mind of the reader. This may not seem fair, but even a minor error—a misspelling or the confusing placement of a comma—will make a much greater impression on your reader than perhaps it should. Remember that everything about your paper is your responsibility, including performing even the supposedly little jobs correctly. Careless editing undermines the effectiveness of your paper. It would be a shame if all the hard work you put into prewriting, drafting, and revising were to be damaged because you carelessly allowed a comma splice!

Most of the revision tips given above hold for editing as well. It is best to edit in stages, looking for only one or two kinds of errors each time you reread the paper. Focus especially on errors that you remember committing in the past. If, for instance, you know that you have a tendency to misplace commas, go through your paper looking at each comma carefully. If you have a weakness for writing unintentional sentence fragments, read each sentence aloud to make sure that it is indeed a complete sentence. Have you accidentally shifted verb tenses anywhere, moving from past to present tense for no reason? Do all the subjects in your sentences agree in number with their verbs? *Now is the time to find out.*

Watch out for *miscues*—problems with a sentence that the writer simply does not see. Remember that your search for errors is hampered in two ways:

1. As the writer, you hope not to find any errors in your work. This desire can cause you to miss mistakes when they do occur.
2. Because you know your material so well, it is easy, as you read, to unconsciously supply missing material—a word, a piece of punctuation—as if it were present.

How difficult is it to see that something is missing in the following sentence?

Unfortunately, school boards often have too little understanding the mental health needs of students.

We can guess that the missing word is probably *of*, which should be inserted after *understanding*. It is quite possible, however, that the writer of the sentence would automatically supply the missing *of* as if it were on the page. This is a miscue, which can be hard for writers to spot because they are so close to their material.

One tactic for catching mistakes in sentence structure is to read the sentences aloud, starting with the last one in the paper and then moving to the next-to-last, then to the previous sentence, and thus going backward through the paper (reading each sentence in the normal, left-to-right manner, of course) until you reach the first sentence of the introduction. This backward progression strips each sentence of its rhetorical context and helps you focus on its internal structure.

Editing is the stage in which you finally answer those minor questions that you had put off when you were wrestling with wording and organization. Any ambiguities regarding the use of abbreviations, italics, numerals, capital letters, titles (when do you capitalize the title *president*, for example?), hyphens, dashes (usually created on a type-writer or computer by striking the hyphen key twice), apostrophes, and quotation marks have to be cleared up now. You must also check to see that you have used the required formats for footnotes, endnotes, margins, page numbers, and the like.

Guessing is not allowed. Sometimes unpracticed writers who realize that they do not quite understand a particular rule of grammar, punctuation, or format do nothing to fill that knowledge gap. Instead they rely on guesswork and their own logic—which is not always up to the task of dealing with so contrary a language as English—to get them through problems that they could solve if they referred to a writing manual. Remember that it does not matter to the reader why or how an error shows up in your writing. It only matters that you have dropped your guard. You must not allow a careless error to undo all the good work that you have done.

Proofread

Before you hand in the final version of your paper, it is vital that you check it one more time to make sure there are no errors of any sort. This job is called *proofreading*, or *proofing*. In essence, you are looking for many of the same things you had checked for during editing, but now you are doing it on the last draft, which is about to be submitted to your audience. Proofreading is as important as editing; you may have missed an error that you still have time to find, or an error may have been introduced when the draft was recopied or typed for the last time. Like every other stage of the writing process, proofreading is your responsibility.

At this point, you must check for typing mistakes: transposed or deleted letters, words, phrases, or punctuation. If you have had the paper professionally typed, you still must check it carefully. Do not rely solely on the typist's proofreading. If you are creating your paper on a computer or a word processor, it is possible for you to unintentionally insert a command that alters your document drastically by slicing out a word, line, or sentence at the touch of a key. Make sure such accidental deletions have not occurred.

Above all else, remember that your paper represents you. It is a product of your best thinking, your most energetic and imaginative response to a writing challenge. If you have maintained your enthusiasm for the project and worked through the stages of the writing process honestly and carefully, you should produce a paper you can be proud of, one that will serve its readers well.

Read&Write 2.3 Discover Your Own Style

The wisdom of the Oracle of Delphi was noted by Socrates, who affirmed the Oracle's belief in the key to wisdom itself: "Know yourself." Fulfilling this admonition can become a lifelong occupation. As psychologists may tell you, helping others know themselves offers a potentially fulfilling career. Write a two-page description of yourself. Be as concise and specific as possible, providing examples of your habits, proclivities, and personality traits. Now, be brave! Share your essay with friends or fellow students. Ask them the extent to which they see you as you see yourself.

3

PRACTICE THE CRAFT

OF SCHOLARSHIP

3.1   THE COMPETENT WRITER

Good writing places your thoughts in your readers' minds in exactly the way you want them to be there. Good writing tells your readers just what you want them to know without telling them anything you do not want them to know. This may sound odd, but the fact is that writers have to be careful not to let unwanted messages slip into their writing. Look, for example, at the passage below, taken from a paper analyzing the impact of a worker-retraining program. Hidden within the prose is a message that jeopardizes the paper's success. Can you detect the message?

> Recent articles written on the subject of brain injuries and cognition have had little to say about the particular problems dealt with in this paper. Because few of these articles focus on the brain injuries resulting from automobile accidents.

Chances are, when you reached the end of the second "sentence," you felt that something was missing and perceived a gap in logic or coherence, so you went back through both sentences to find the place where things had gone wrong. The text following the first sentence is actually not a sentence at all. It does have certain features of a sentence—for example, a subject (*few*) and a verb (*focus*)—but its first word (*Because*) subordinates the entire clause that follows, taking away its ability to stand on its own as a complete idea. The second "sentence," which is properly called a *subordinate clause*, merely fills in some information about the first sentence, telling us why recent articles about dislocated workers fail to deal with problems discussed in the present paper.

The sort of error represented by the second "sentence" is commonly called a *sentence fragment*, and it conveys to the reader a message that no writer wants to send: that the writer either is careless or, worse, has not mastered the language. Language errors such as fragments, misplaced commas, or shifts in verb tense send out warnings in readers' minds. As a result, readers lose some of their concentration on the issue being discussed; they become distracted and begin to wonder about the language competency of the writer. The writing loses effectiveness.

> **Note:** Whatever goal you set for your paper—whether to persuade, describe, analyze, or speculate—you must also set one other goal: to display language competence. If your paper does not meet this goal, it will not completely achieve its other aims. Language errors spread doubt like a virus; they jeopardize all the hard work you have done on your paper.

Language competence is important in psychology, for credibility in science depends on accuracy in communication.

Correctness Is Relative

Although they may seem minor, the sort of language errors we are discussing—often called *surface errors*—can be extremely damaging in certain kinds of writing. Surface errors come in a variety of types, including misspellings, punctuation problems, grammar errors, and the inconsistent use of abbreviations, capitalization, and numerals. These errors are an affront to your readers' notion of correctness, and therein lies one of the biggest problems with surface errors. Different audiences tolerate different levels of correctness. You know that you can get away with surface errors in, say, a letter to a friend, who will probably not judge you harshly for them, whereas those same errors in a job application letter might eliminate you from consideration for the position. Correctness depends to an extent on context.

Another problem is that the rules governing correctness shift over time. What would have been an error to your grandmother's generation—the splitting of an infinitive, for example, or the ending of a sentence with a preposition—is taken in stride by most readers today.

So how do you write correctly when the rules shift from person to person and over time? Here are some tips.

Consider Your Audience   One of the great risks of writing is that even the simplest of choices regarding wording or punctuation can sometimes prejudice your audience against you in ways that may seem unfair. For example, look again at the old grammar rule forbidding the splitting of infinitives. After decades of telling students to never split an infinitive (something just done in this sentence), most composition experts now concede that a split infinitive is *not* a grammar crime. Now, as a college student, your primary audience is group of professors who teach your courses. Suppose you have written a paper trying to affirm that new research in adolescent psychology unduly reflects racial bias. How will your professor, who has published in scholarly journals for a quarter century, respond when you say, in your introduction, that research on adolescents "needs to always include" a focus on more minority and poor populations? How much of the professor's attention have you suddenly lost because of his or her automatic recollection of what is now a nonrule about splitting an infinitive?

It is possible, in other words, to write correctly and still offend your readers' notions of language competence.

Make sure that you tailor the surface features and the degree of formality of your writing to the level of competency that your readers require. When in doubt, take a conservative approach. Don't get careless, because you'll find your audience might be just as distracted by a contraction as by a split infinitive.

Aim for Consistency   When dealing with a language question for which there are different answers—such as whether to use a comma before the conjunction in a series of three (*the professor's lecture addressed learning styles, memory cues, and methods of maintaining attention*)—always use the same strategy throughout your paper. If, for example, you avoid splitting one infinitive, avoid splitting *all* infinitives.

Have Confidence in What You Know about Writing!

It is easy for unpracticed writers to allow their occasional mistakes to shake their confidence in their writing ability. The fact is, however, that most of what we know about writing is correct. We are all capable, for example, of writing grammatically sound phrases, even if we cannot list the rules by which we achieve coherence. Most writers who worry about their chronic errors make fewer mistakes than they think. Becoming distressed about errors makes writing even more difficult.

Read&Write 3.1   Correct a Sentence Fragment

See how many ways you can rewrite this so-called two-sentence passage to eliminate the fragment and make the passage syntactically correct:

Although married couples often both work full-time, women do most of the house-work. Except when the men work second or third shifts.

3.2   AVOID ERRORS IN GRAMMAR AND PUNCTUATION

As various composition theorists have pointed out, the word *grammar* has several definitions. One meaning is "the formal patterns in which words must be arranged in order to convey meaning." We learn these patterns very early in life and use them spontaneously, without thinking. Our understanding of grammatical patterns is extremely sophisticated, despite the fact that few of us can actually cite the rules by which the patterns work. Patrick Hartwell tested grammar learning by asking native English speakers of different ages and levels of education, including high school teachers, to arrange these words in natural order:

French the young girls four

Everyone could produce the natural order for this phrase: *the four young French girls.* Yet none of Hartwell's respondents was able to cite the rules that govern the order of the words.[1]

---

[1]   Hartwell, P. (1985). Grammar, grammars, and the teaching of grammar. *College English, 47,* 105–127.

Eliminate Chronic Errors   But if just thinking about our errors has a negative effect on our writing, how do we learn to write more correctly? Perhaps the best answer is simply to write as often as possible. Give yourself lots of practice in putting your thoughts into written shape and then in revising and proofing your work. As you write and revise, be honest—and patient—with yourself. Chronic errors are like bad habits; getting rid of them takes time.

You probably know of one or two problem areas in your writing that you could have eliminated but have not yet done so. Instead, you may have fudged your writing at the critical points, relying on half-remembered formulas from past English classes or trying to come up with logical solutions to your writing problems. (*Reminder:* The English language does not always work in a way that seems logical.) You may have simply decided that comma rules are unlearnable or that you will never understand the difference between the verbs *lay* and *lie*. And so you guess, and you come up with the wrong answer a good part of the time. What a shame, when just a little extra work would give you mastery over those few gaps in your understanding and boost your confidence as well.

Instead of continuing with this sort of guesswork and living with the holes in your knowledge, why not face the problem areas now and learn the rules that have heretofore escaped you? What follows is a discussion of those surface features of writing in which errors most commonly occur. You will probably be familiar with most if not all of the rules discussed, but there may well be a few you have not yet mastered. Now is the time to do so.

Apostrophes

An apostrophe is used to show possession. When you wish to say that something belongs to someone or something, you add either an apostrophe and an *s* or an apostrophe alone to the word that represents the owner.

1. When the owner is singular (a single person or thing), the apostrophe precedes an added *s*:

   According to CEO Anderson's secretary, the senior staff meeting has been canceled.

   The union's lawyers challenged the government's policy in court.

   Somebody's briefcase was left in the auditorium.

2. The same rule applies if the word showing possession is a plural that does not end in *s*:

   The women's club sponsored several benefit concerts during their annual charity drive.

   Father Garrity has proven himself a tireless worker for improved children's services.

3. When the word expressing ownership is a plural ending in *s*, the apostrophe follows the *s*:

   The new initiation ceremony was discussed at the club secretaries' conference.

There are two ways to form the possessive for two or more nouns.

1. To show joint possession (both nouns owning the same thing or things), only the last noun in the series is possessive:

    The therapist and his assistant's invitations were sent out yesterday.

2. To indicate that each noun owns an item or items individually, each noun must show possession:

    Superintendent Scott's and Principal MacKay's speeches took different approaches to the same problem.

The importance of the apostrophe is obvious when you consider the difference in meaning between the following two sentences:

Be sure to pick up the volunteer's bags on your way to the airport.

Be sure to pick up the volunteers' bags on your way to the airport.

In the first sentence, you have only one volunteer to worry about, whereas in the second, you have at least two!

Capitalization

Here is a brief summary of some hard-to-remember capitalization rules:

1. You may, if you choose, capitalize the first letter of the first word in a sentence that follows a colon. However, make sure you use one pattern consistently throughout your paper:

    Our instructions are explicit: *Do not* allow anyone into the conference without an identification badge.

    Our instructions are explicit: *do not* allow anyone into the conference without an identification badge.

2. Capitalize *proper nouns* (names of specific people, places, or things) and *proper adjectives* (adjectives made from proper nouns). A common noun following a proper adjective is usually not capitalized, nor is a common adjective (such as *a*, *an*, or *the*) preceding a proper adjective:

Proper Nouns	Proper Adjectives
Poland	Polish officials
Iraq	the Iraqi ambassador
Shakespeare	a Shakespearean tragedy

Proper nouns include:

- *Names of monuments and buildings:* the Washington Monument, the Empire State Building, the Library of Congress
- *Historical events, eras, and certain terms concerning calendar dates:* the Civil War, the Dark Ages, Monday, December, Columbus Day
- *Parts of the country:* North, Southwest, Eastern Seaboard, the West Coast, New England.

> **Note:** When words like *north*, *south*, *east*, *west*, and *northwest* are used to designate direction rather than geographical region, they are not capitalized: *We drove east to Boston and then made a tour of the East Coast.*

- *Words referring to race, psychology, and nationality:* Islam, Muslim, Caucasian, White (or white), Asian, Negro, Black (or black), Slavic, Arab, Jewish, Hebrew, Buddhism, Buddhists, Southern Baptists, the Bible, the Koran, American
- *Names of languages:* English, Chinese, Latin, Sanskrit
- *Titles of corporations, institutions, universities, and organizations:* Dow Chemical, General Motors, the National Endowment for the Humanities, University of Tennessee, Colby College, Kiwanis Club, American Association of Retired Persons, Oklahoma State Senate

> **Note:** Some words once considered proper nouns or adjectives have, over time, become common and are no longer capitalized, such as *french fries*, *pasteurized milk*, *arabic numerals*, and *italics*.

3. Titles of individuals may be capitalized if they precede a proper name; otherwise, titles are usually not capitalized:

The committee honored Senator Jones.
The committee honored the senator from Kansas.
We phoned Doctor Jessup, who arrived shortly afterward.
We phoned the doctor, who arrived shortly afterward.
A story on Queen Elizabeth's health appeared in yesterday's paper.
A story on the queen's health appeared in yesterday's paper.
Pope Francis's visit to Colorado was a public relations success.
The pope's visit to Colorado was a public relations success.

When Not to Capitalize In general, you do not capitalize nouns when your reference is nonspecific. For example, you would not capitalize *the senator*, but you would capitalize *Senator Smith*. The second reference is as much a title as it is a term of identification, whereas the first reference is a mere identifier. Likewise, there is a difference in degree of specificity between *the state treasury* and *the Texas State Treasury*.

> **Note:** The meaning of a term may change somewhat depending on its capitalization. What, for example, might be the difference between a *Democrat* and a *democrat*? When capitalized, the word refers to a member of a specific political party; when not capitalized, it refers to someone who believes in the democratic form of government.

Capitalization depends to some extent on the context of your writing. For example, if you are writing a policy analysis for a specific corporation, you may capitalize words and phrases that refer to that corporation—such as *Board of Directors*,

Chairman of the Board, and *the Institute* —that would not be capitalized in a paper written for a more general audience. Likewise, in some contexts, it is not unusual to see the titles of certain powerful officials capitalized even when not accompanying a proper noun:

> The President took few members of his staff to Camp David with him.

Colons

We all know certain uses for the colon. A colon can, for example, separate the parts of a statement of time (*4:25 a.m.*), separate chapter and verse in a biblical quotation (*John 3:16*), and close the salutation of a business letter (*Dear Director Keaton:*). But the colon has other, less well-known uses that can add extra flexibility to sentence structure.

The colon can introduce into a sentence certain kinds of material, such as a list, a quotation, or a restatement or description of material mentioned earlier:

List

> The committee's research proposal promised to do three things: (1) establish the extent of the problem, (2) examine several possible solutions, and (3) estimate the cost of each solution.

Quotation

> In his lecture, the psychiatrist challenged us with these words: "How will your personal attitudes make a difference in the life of our city?"

Restatement or description

> Ahead of us, according to the hospital's chief of staff, lay the biggest job of all: convincing our patients of the plan's benefits.

Commas

The comma is perhaps the most troublesome of all marks of punctuation, no doubt because its use is governed by so many variables, such as sentence length, rhetorical emphasis, and changing notions of style. The most common problems are outlined below.

The Comma Splice   A *comma splice* is the joining of two complete sentences with only a comma:

> The patient told us his therapist diagnosed his condition after only two sessions, the therapist's report says the diagnosis took much longer.

> An unemployed worker who has been effectively retrained is no longer an economic problem for the community, he has become an asset.

> It might be possible for the city to assess fees on the sale of real estate, however, such a move would be criticized by the community of real estate developers.

In each of these passages, two complete sentences (also called *independent clauses*) have been spliced together by only a comma, which is an inadequate break between the two sentences.

One foolproof way to check your paper for comma splices is to read the structures on both sides of each comma carefully. If you find a complete sentence on each side, and if the sentence following the comma does not begin with a coordinating conjunction (*and, but, for, nor, or, so, yet*), then you have found a comma splice.

Simply reading the draft to try to "hear" the comma splices may not work because the rhetorical features of your prose—its *movement*—may make it hard to detect this kind of error in sentence completeness. There are five commonly used ways to correct comma splices:

1. Place a period between the two independent clauses:

   INCORRECT A psychologist receives many benefits from his or her affiliation with a political hospital, there are liabilities as well.

   CORRECT A psychologist receives many benefits from his or her affiliation with a hospital. There are liabilities as well.

2. Place a comma and a coordinating conjunction (*and, but, for, or, nor, so, yet*) between the independent clauses:

   INCORRECT The psychotherapist's speech described the major differences of opinion over behavior modification techniques, it also suggested areas of common agreement.

   CORRECT The psychotherapist's speech described the major differences of opinion over behavior modification techniques, and it also suggested areas of common agreement.

3. Place a semicolon between the independent clauses:

   INCORRECT Some people feel that spanking has a proper role in child raising, many others disagree.

   CORRECT Some people feel that spanking has a proper role in child raising; many others disagree.

4. Rewrite the two clauses as one independent clause:

   INCORRECT Television ads played a big part in selling antidepressants, however they were not the deciding factor in the challenger's victory over the incumbent.

   CORRECT Television ads played a large but not a decisive role in selling antidepressants.

5. Change one of the independent clauses into a dependent clause by beginning it with a subordinating word (*although, after, as, because, before, if, though, unless, when, which, where*), which prevents the clause from being able to stand on its own as a complete sentence.

   INCORRECT The therapy session ended last Tuesday, the client reported substantial improvement.

   CORRECT When the therapy session ended last Tuesday, the client reported substantial improvement.

Commas in a Compound Sentence A *compound sentence* is composed of two or more independent clauses—that is, two complete sentences. When these two clauses are joined by a coordinating conjunction, the conjunction should be preceded by a comma to signal the reader that another independent clause follows. (This is method 2 for fixing a comma splice, described above.) When the comma is missing, the reader is not expecting to find the second half of a compound sentence and may be distracted from the text.

As the following examples indicate, the missing comma is especially a problem in longer sentences or in sentences in which other coordinating conjunctions appear. Notice how the comma sorts out the two main parts of the compound sentence, eliminating confusion:

INCORRECT | Dr. Winthrop promised to visit the hospital and investigate the problem and then he called the press conference to a close.

CORRECT | Dr. Winthrop promised to visit the hospital and investigate the problem, and then he called the press conference to a close.

INCORRECT | The water board can neither make policy nor enforce it nor can its members serve on auxiliary water committees.

CORRECT | The water board can neither make policy nor enforce it, nor can its members serve on auxiliary water committees.

An exception to this rule arises in shorter sentences, where the comma may not be necessary to make the meaning clear:

The executive director phoned and we thanked him for his support.

However, it is never wrong to place a comma after the conjunction between independent clauses. If you are the least bit unsure of your audience's notion of "proper" grammar, it is a good idea to take the conservative approach and use the comma:

The executive director phoned, and we thanked him for his support.

Commas with Restrictive and Nonrestrictive Elements A *nonrestrictive element* is a part of a sentence—a word, phrase, or clause—that adds information about another element in the sentence without restricting or limiting its meaning. Although this information may be useful, the nonrestrictive element is not needed for the sentence to make sense. To signal its inessential nature, the nonrestrictive element is set off from the rest of the sentence with commas.

The failure to use commas to indicate the nonrestrictive nature of a sentence element can cause confusion. See, for example, how the presence or absence of commas affects our understanding of the following sentence:

The psychiatrist was talking with the psychotherapist, who won the outstanding service award last year.

The psychiatrist was talking with the psychotherapist who won the outstanding service award last year.

Can you see that the comma changes the meaning of the sentence? In the first version of the sentence, the comma makes the information that follows it incidental:

The psychiatrist was talking with the psychotherapist, who happened to have won the service award last year. In the second version of the sentence, the information following the word *psychotherapist* is vital to the sense of the sentence; it tells us specifically *which* psychotherapist—presumably there are more than one—the psychology professor was addressing. Here, the lack of a comma has transformed the material following the word *psychotherapist* into a *restrictive element*, which means that it is necessary to our understanding of the sentence.

Be sure that you make a clear distinction in your paper between nonrestrictive and restrictive elements by setting off the nonrestrictive elements with commas.

Commas in a Series   A series is any two or more items of a similar nature that appear consecutively in a sentence. These items may be individual words, phrases, or clauses. In a series of three or more items, the items are separated by commas:

> The butler, the baker, and the chauffeur all attended the ceremony.

> Because of the new zoning regulations, all trailer parks must be moved out of the neighborhood, all small businesses must apply for recertification and tax status, and the two local churches must repave their parking lots.

The final comma in the series, the one before *and*, is sometimes left out, especially in newspaper writing. This practice, however, can make for confusion, especially in longer, complicated sentences like the second example above. Here is the way this sentence would read without the final, or serial, comma:

> Because of the new zoning regulations, all trailer parks must be moved out of the neighborhood, all small businesses must apply for recertification and tax status and the two local churches must repave their parking lots.

Notice that, without a comma, the division between the second and third items in the series is not clear. This is the sort of ambiguous structure that can cause a reader to backtrack and lose concentration. You can avoid such confusion by always using that final comma. Remember, however, that if you do decide to include it, do so consistently; make sure it appears in every series in your paper.

Misplaced Modifiers

A *modifier* is a word or group of words used to describe, or modify, another word in the sentence. A *misplaced modifier*, sometimes called a dangling modifier, appears at either the beginning or the end of a sentence and seems to be describing some word other than the one the writer obviously intended. The modifier therefore "dangles," disconnected from what it truly modifies. It is often hard for the writer to spot dangling modifiers, but readers can—and will—find them, and the result can be disastrous for the sentence, as the following examples demonstrate:

INCORRECT   Flying low over Beverly Hills, Oral Roberts' mansion was seen.

CORRECT   Flying low over Beverly Hills, we saw Oral Roberts' Mansion.

INCORRECT	Worried at the cost of the menu, the dessert was eliminated by the committee.
CORRECT	Worried at the cost of the menu, the committee eliminated the dessert.
INCORRECT	To lobby for improved mental health services, a lot of effort went into the television ads.
CORRECT	The lobby group put a lot of effort into the television ads for improved mental health services.
INCORRECT	Stunned, the television broadcast the defeated senator's concession speech.
CORRECT	The television broadcast the stunned senator's concession speech.

Note that, in the first two incorrect sentences above, the confusion is largely due to the use of *passive-voice* verbs: "Oral Roberts' mansion *was seen*"; "the dessert *was eliminated.*" Often, although not always, a dangling modifier results because the actor in the sentence—*we* in the first sentence, *the committee* in the second—is either distanced from the modifier or obliterated by the passive-voice verb. It is a good idea to avoid using the passive voice unless you have a specific reason for doing so.

One way to check for dangling modifiers is to examine all modifiers at the beginning or end of your sentences. Look especially for *to be* phrases or for words ending in *-ing* or *-ed* at the start of the modifier. Then see if the modified word is close enough to the phrase to be properly connected.

Parallelism

Series of two or more words, phrases, or clauses within a sentence should have the same grammatical structure, a situation called *parallelism*. Parallel structures can add power and balance to your writing by creating a strong rhetorical rhythm. Pastors and politicians are particularly fond of them. Here is a famous example of parallelism from the preamble to the U.S. Constitution (the capitalization follows that of the original eighteenth-century document. Parallel structures have been italicized):

> We the People of the United States, in Order to *form a more perfect Union, establish Justice, insure domestic Tranquillity, provide for the common defence, promote the general Welfare,* and *secure the Blessings of Liberty* to ourselves and our Posterity, do *ordain* and *establish* this Constitution for the United States of America.

There are actually two series in this sentence: the first, composed of six phrases, each of which completes the infinitive phrase beginning with the word *to* (*to form,* [*to*] *establish,* [*to*] *insure,* [*to*] *provide,* [*to*] *promote,* and [*to*] *secure*); the second, consisting of two verbs (*ordain* and *establish*). These parallel series appeal to our love of balance and pattern, and they give an authoritative tone to the sentence. The writer, we feel, has thought long and carefully about the matter at hand and has taken firm control of it.

Because we find a special satisfaction in balanced structures, we are more likely to remember ideas phrased in parallelisms than in less highly ordered language. For this reason, as well as for the sense of authority and control that they suggest, parallel structures are common in political utterances:

> *We hold these truths to be self-evident, that all men are created equal, that they are endowed by their Creator with certain unalienable rights, that among these are life, liberty, and the pursuit of happiness.*
>
> —The Declaration of Independence, 1776

> *But in a larger sense, we cannot dedicate, we cannot consecrate, we cannot hallow this ground.*
>
> —Abraham Lincoln, Gettysburg Address, 1863

Faulty Parallelism   If the parallelism of a passage is not carefully maintained, the writing can seem sloppy and out of balance. Scan your writing to make sure that all series and lists have parallel structures. The following examples show how to correct faulty parallelism:

INCORRECT	The patient care director promises not only *to reform* the human resources department but also *the giving of raises* to all hospital employees. (Connective structures such as *not only . . . but also* and *both . . . and* introduce elements that should be parallel.)
CORRECT	The patient care director promises not only *to reform* the human resources department but also *to give* raises to all hospital employees.
INCORRECT	The cost *of doing nothing* is greater than the cost *to renovate* the emergency room.
CORRECT	The cost *of doing nothing* is greater than the cost *of renovating* the emergency room.
INCORRECT	Here are the items on the committee's agenda: (1) *to discuss* the new treatment methods, (2) *to revise* the wording of the treatment protocol, (3) *a vote* on the director's request for an assistant.
CORRECT	Here are the items on the committee's agenda: (1) *to discuss* the new treatment methods, (2) *to revise* the wording of the treatment protocol, (3) *to vote* on the director's request for an assistant.

Fused (Run-On) Sentences

A *fused sentence* is one in which two or more independent clauses (passages that can stand as complete sentences) have been run together without the aid of any suitable connecting word, phrase, or punctuation. There are several ways to correct a fused sentence:

INCORRECT	The recidivism committee members were exhausted they had debated for two hours.

CORRECT	The recidivism committee members were exhausted. They had debated for two hours. (The clauses have been separated into two sentences.)
CORRECT	The recidivism committee members were exhausted; they had debated for two hours. (The clauses have been separated by a semicolon.)
CORRECT	The recidivism committee members were exhausted, having debated for two hours. (The second clause has been rephrased as a dependent clause.)
INCORRECT	Our policy analysis impressed the committee it also convinced them to reconsider their action.
CORRECT	Our policy recommendations impressed the committee and also convinced them to reconsider their action. (The second clause has been rephrased as part of the first clause.)
CORRECT	Our policy recommendation impressed the committee, and it also convinced them to reconsider their action. (The clauses have been separated by a comma and a coordinating word.)

Although a fused sentence is easily noticeable to the reader, it can be maddeningly difficult for the writer to catch. Unpracticed writers tend to read through the fused spots, sometimes mentally supplying the break that is usually heard when sentences are spoken. To check for fused sentences, read the independent clauses in your paper carefully, making sure that there are adequate breaks among all of them.

Pronouns

Its **Versus** *It's*   Do not make the mistake of trying to form the possessive of *it* in the same way that you form the possessive of most nouns. The pronoun *it* shows possession by simply adding an *s*:

The psychologist assessed the case on its merits.

The word *it's* is a contraction of *it is*:

It's the most expensive program ever launched by the behavioral research center.

What makes the *its/it's* rule so confusing is that most nouns form the singular possessive by adding an apostrophe and an *s*:

The psychologist's diagnosis startled her client.

When proofreading, any time you come to the word *it's*, substitute the phrase *it is* while you read. If the phrase makes sense, you have used the correct form. If you have used the word *it's*:

The newspaper article was misleading in *it's* analysis of the mental health crisis.

then read it as *it is*:

> The newspaper article was misleading in *it is* analysis of the mental health crisis.

If the phrase makes no sense, substitute *its* for *it's*:

> The newspaper article was misleading in *its* analysis of the mental health crisis.

Vague Pronoun References   Pronouns are words that take the place of nouns or other pronouns that have already been mentioned in your writing. The most common pronouns include *he, she, it, they, them, those, which,* and *who*. You must make sure there is no confusion about the word to which each pronoun refers:

> The psychology professor said that he would support our research proposal if the dean would also back it.

The word that the pronoun replaces is called its *antecedent*. To check the accuracy of your pronoun references, ask yourself, "To what does the pronoun refer?" Then answer the question carefully, making sure that there is not more than one possible antecedent. Consider the following example:

> Several special interest groups decided to defeat the new health care bill. This became the turning point of the government's reform campaign.

To what does the word *this* refer? The immediate answer seems to be the word *bill* at the end of the previous sentence. It is more likely, however, that the writer was referring to the attempt of the special interest groups to defeat the bill, but there is no word in the first sentence that refers specifically to this action. The pronoun reference is thus unclear. One way to clarify the reference is to change the beginning of the second sentence:

> Several special interest groups decided to defeat the new health care bill. Their attack on the bill became the turning point of the government's reform campaign.

Here is another example:

> When John F. Kennedy appointed his brother Robert to the position of U.S. attorney general, he had little idea how widespread the corruption in the Teamsters Union was.

To whom does the word *he* refer? It is unclear whether the writer is referring to John or Robert Kennedy. One way to clarify the reference is simply to repeat the antecedent instead of using a pronoun:

> When John F. Kennedy appointed his brother Robert to the position of U.S. attorney general, Robert had little idea how widespread the corruption in the Teamsters Union was.

Pronoun Agreement   A pronoun must agree with its antecedent in both gender and number, as the following examples demonstrate:

> Bank manager Smith said that he appreciated our club's support in the fundraising campaign.

One reporter asked the researcher what she would do if the clinic offered her a promotion.

Having listened to our proposal, the director decided to put it into effect within the week.

Therapists working with the injured motorist said they were pleased with her recovery so far.

Certain words, however, can be troublesome antecedents because they may look like plural pronouns but are actually singular:

anyone	each	either	everybody	everyone
nobody	no one	somebody	someone	

A pronoun referring to one of these words in a sentence must be singular, too:

INCORRECT	Each of the women in the support group brought their children.
CORRECT	Each of the women in the support group brought her children.
INCORRECT	Has everybody received their medication?
CORRECT	Has everybody received his or her medication? (The two gender-specific pronouns are used to avoid sexist language.)
CORRECT	Have all the patients received their medications? (The singular antecedent has been changed to a plural one.)

A Shift in Person

It is important to avoid shifting unnecessarily among first person (*I*, *we*, and sometimes *one*), second person (*you*), and third person (*she*, *he*, *it*, *one*, *they*). Such shifts can cause confusion:

INCORRECT	Most people (third person) who attend counseling sessions find that if you (second person) tell the truth during your session, you will benefit from the session.
CORRECT	Most people who attend counseling sessions find that if they tell the truth during their sessions, they will benefit from the sessions.
INCORRECT	One (first person) cannot tell whether you (second person) are suited for scientific research until they decide to try it.
CORRECT	One cannot tell whether one is suited for scientific research until one decides to try it.

Quotation Marks

It can be difficult to remember when to use quotation marks and where they go in relation to other punctuation. When faced with these questions, unpracticed writers often try to rely on logic rather than on a rule book, but the rules do not always seem to rely on logic. The only way to make sure of your use of quotation marks is to memorize the rules. Luckily, there are not many.

Use quotation marks to enclose direct quotations that are no longer than 100 words or eight typed lines:

> In his farewell address to the staff of the counseling agency, the client lamented, "Bad jokes can take all the fun out of good therapy."

Longer quotations, called *block quotations*, are placed in a double-spaced indented block, without quotation marks:

> In a response to his insurance company's letter, the client clearly attributed his deteriorating condition to his therapist's incompetence:
>
> > I am only thirty-five years old, and I look like I have been president of the United States for the last eight years. Look at my hair! It's all white! I'm lucky to have any hair left after what he did to my nerves. The guy's native language is from Comedy Central! He filled my expensive sessions with puns and bad jokes, and, on top of it all, he kept calling me "Shirley." Now I'm popping pills just to sleep at night. I walk the dog six times a day, even though it's not my dog. I cry so much my mother asked me to move out of her house. It's February, and I don't even have a sleeping bag, much less a tent.

Use single quotation marks to set off quotations within quotations:

> "I intend," said the client, "to write on my evaluation form a line from Edward Arlington Robinson's poem, 'Richard Cory.'"

Note: When the quote occurs at the end of the sentence, as in the example above, both the single and double quotation marks are placed outside the period.

Use quotation marks to set off titles of the following:

Short poems (those not printed as a separate volume)
Short stories
Articles or essays
Songs
Episodes of television or radio shows

Use quotation marks to set off words or phrases used in special ways:

- To convey irony:

  > This "humane" policy of the hospital administration has resulted in a drastic increase of patient complaints.

- To indicate a technical term:

  > To "filibuster" is to delay legislation, usually through prolonged speech-making. The last notable filibuster occurred just last week in the Senate.

  (Once the term is defined, it is not placed in quotation marks again.)

Quotation Marks in Relation to Other Punctuation   Place commas and periods *inside* closing quotation marks:

> "My fellow skilled helpers," said the psychologist, "there is plenty of work ahead of us."

Place colons and semicolons *outside* closing quotation marks:

> In his speech on voting, the professor warned against "an encroaching indolence"; he was referring to his abnormal-psychology class.

> There are several victims of the college president's campaign to "Turn Back the Deficit": cafeteria workers, gardeners, the mentally impaired.

Use the context to determine whether to place question marks, exclamation points, and dashes inside or outside closing quotation marks. If the punctuation is part of the quotation, place it inside the quotation mark:

> "When will my therapist make up her mind?" asked the retired pugilist.

> The retirement home residents shouted, "Free the hostages!" and "No more slavery!"

If the punctuation is not part of the quotation, place it outside the quotation mark:

> Which Democratic candidate said, "We have nothing to fear but fear itself"?

Note that although the quote in this last example is a complete sentence, you do not place a period after it. There can only be one piece of *terminal punctuation* (punctuation that ends a sentence).

Semicolons

The semicolon is a little-used punctuation mark that you should learn to incorporate into your writing strategy because of its many potential applications. For example, a semicolon can be used to correct a comma splice:

INCORRECT	The mental health team members left the meeting in good spirits, their demands were met.
CORRECT	The mental health team members left the meeting in good spirits; their demands were met.
INCORRECT	Several guests at the fundraiser had lost their invitations, however, we were able to seat them anyway.
CORRECT	Several guests at the fundraiser had lost their invitations; however, we were able to seat them anyway.

It is important to remember that conjunctive adverbs such as *however, therefore,* and *thus* are not coordinating words (such as *and, but, or, for, so, yet*) and cannot be used with a comma to link independent clauses. If the second independent clause begins with *however,* it must be preceded by either a period or a semicolon. As you can see from the second example above, connecting two independent clauses with

council/counsel
dairy/diary
descent/dissent
desert/dessert
device/devise
die/dye
dominant/dominate
elicit/illicit
eminent/immanent/
  imminent

moral/morale
of/off
passed/past
patience/patients
peace/piece
personal/personnel
plain/plane
precede/proceed
presence/presents

track/tract
waist/waste
waive/wave
weak/week
weather/whether
were/where
which/witch
whose/who's
your/you're

Commonly Misspelled Words

acceptable
accessible
accommodate
accompany
accustomed
acquire
against
annihilate
apparent
arguing
argument
authentic
before
begin
beginning
believe
benefited
bulletin
business
cannot
category
committee
condemn
courteous
definitely
dependent
desperate
develop
different
disappear
disappoint
easily
efficient
environment
equipped
exceed
exercise
existence

hypocrite
ideally
immediately
immense
incredible
innocuous
intercede
interrupt
irrelevant
irresistible
irritate
knowledge
license
likelihood
maintenance
manageable
meanness
millennial
mischievous
missile
necessary
nevertheless
no one
noticeable
noticing
nuisance
occasion
occasionally
occurred
occurrences
omission
omit
opinion
opponent
parallel
parole
peaceable
performance

received
recession
recommend
referring
religious
remembrance
reminisce
repetition
representative
rhythm
ridiculous
roommate
satellite
scarcity
scenery
science
secede
secession
secretary
senseless
separate
sergeant
shining
significant
sincerely
skiing
stubbornness
studying
succeed
success
successfully
susceptible
suspicious
technical
temporary
tendency
therefore
tragedy

experience	pertain	truly
fascinate	practical	tyranny
finally	preparation	unanimous
foresee	probably	unconscious
forty	process	undoubtedly
fulfill	professor	until
gauge	prominent	vacuum
guaranteed	pronunciation	valuable
guard	psychology	various
harass	publicly	vegetable
hero	pursue	visible
heroes	pursuing	without
humorous	questionnaire	women
hurried	realize	
hurriedly	receipt	

Read&Write 3.2 Proofread the Mental Health Bill

Although government agencies provide a wide variety of mental health services and programs, the political process produces gaps and inefficiencies in the system. Legislation is often introduced in Congress to remedy these problems. You will find one such piece of legislation below. Your task is to read the bill and identify and correct 12 errors of grammar and/or punctuation. You will encounter the error-filled bill first. Read it to see how many of the errors you can find. You will then find an error key, and, finally, an error-free version of the bill.

Selections from U.S. Representative Fortney Pete Stark's speech in the House of Representatives on Friday, March 23, 2007, titled INTRODUCING THE MEDICARE MENTAL HEALTH MODERNIZATION ACT [with errors embedded in the text]

Mr. STARK. Madam Speaker, I rise today with my colleagues Jim Ramstad of Minnesota and Patrick Kennedy from Rhode Island to introduce the Medicare Mental Health Modernization Act, a bill to provide mental health parity in Medicare. I have introduced a version of this bill in every Congress since 1994, perhaps this time we can actually enact it.

Medicare's mental health benefit is fashioned on treatments provided in 1965, but mental health care has changed dramatically over the last 42 years. Medicare limits inpatient coverage at psychiatric hospitals to 190 days over an individual's lifetime. In addition, beneficiaries are charged a discriminatory 50 percent coinsurance for outpatient psychotherapy services. Compared to 20 percent for physical health services.

The Medicare Mental Health Modernization Act eliminate this blatant mental health discrimination under Medicare and modernizes the Medicare mental health benefit to meet todays' standards of care.

This bill is long overdue, one in five members of our senior population display mental difficulties that are not part of the normal aging process. In primary care settings, more than a third of senior citizens demonstrate symptoms of depression and impaired social functioning. Yet only one out of every three mentally ill seniors receives the mental health services he/she need. Older adults also has one of the highest rates of suicide of any segment of our population. In addition, mental illness is the single largest diagnostic category for Medicare beneficiaries who qualify as disabled . . .

The Medicare Mental Health Modernization Act is a straightforward bill that improve Medicare's mental health benefits as follows:

It reduces the discriminatory co-payment for outpatient mental health services. From 50 percent to the 20 percent level charged for most other Part B medical services.

It eliminates the arbitrary 190-day lifetime cap on inpatient services in psychiatric hospitals.

It improves beneficiary access to mental health services by including within Medicare a number of community-based residential and intensive outpatient mental health services that characterizes today's state-of-the-art clinical practices.

It further improves access to needed mental health services by addressing the shortage of qualified mental health professionals serving older and disabled Americans in rural and other medically underserved areas. By allowing state licensed marriage and family therapists and mental health counselors to provide Medicare-covered services.

Similarly, it corrects a legislative oversight that will facilitate the provision of mental health services by clinical social workers within skilled nursing facilities.

Key to "Find the Errors"

The letters, words, and punctuation underlined below indicate locations of errors. You can also check the original, error-free copy to find the correct forms of grammar and usage.

INTRODUCING THE MEDICARE MENTAL HEALTH MODERNIZATION ACT (Abridged) [with errors underlined]

Mr. STARK. Madam Speaker, I rise today with my colleagues Jim Ramstad of Minnesota and Patrick Kennedy from Rhode Island to introduce the Medicare Mental Health Modernization Act, a bill to provide mental health parity in Medicare. I have introduced a version of this bill in every Congress since 1994, perhaps this time we can actually enact it.

Medicare's mental health benefit is fashioned on treatments provided in 1965, but mental health care has changed dramatically over the last 42 years. Medicare limits inpatient coverage at psychiatric hospitals to 190 days over an individual's lifetime. In addition, beneficiaries are charged a discriminatory 50 percent coinsurance for outpatient psychotherapy services. Compared to 20 percent for physical health services.

The Medicare Mental Health Modernization Act eliminate this blatant mental health discrimination under Medicare and modernizes the Medicare mental health benefit to meet todays' standards of care.

This bill is long overdue, one in five members of our senior population display mental difficulties that are not part of the normal aging process. In primary care settings, more than a third of senior citizens demonstrate symptoms of depression and impaired social functioning. Yet only one out of every three mentally ill seniors receives the mental health services he/she <u>need</u>. Older adults also <u>has</u> one of the highest rates of suicide of any segment of our population. In addition, mental illness is the single largest diagnostic category for Medicare beneficiaries who qualify as disabled . . .

The Medicare Mental Health Modernization Act is a straightforward bill that <u>improve</u> Medicare's mental health benefits as follows:

It reduces the discriminatory co-payment for outpatient mental health <u>services.</u> <u>From</u> 50 percent to the 20 percent level charged for most other Part B medical services.

It eliminates the arbitrary 190-day lifetime cap on inpatient services in psychiatric hospitals.

It improves beneficiary access to mental health services by including within Medicare a number of community-based residential and intensive outpatient mental health services that <u>characterizes</u> today's state-of-the-art clinical practices.

It further improves access to needed mental health services by addressing the shortage of qualified mental health professionals serving older and disabled Americans in rural and other medically underserved <u>areas. By</u> allowing state licensed marriage and family therapists and mental health counselors to provide Medicare-covered services.

Similarly, it corrects a legislative oversight that will facilitate the provision of mental health services by clinical social workers within skilled nursing facilities.

INTRODUCING THE MEDICARE MENTAL HEALTH MODERNIZATION ACT (Abridged) [original speech without errors]

Mr. STARK. Madam Speaker, I rise today with my colleagues Jim Ramstad of Minnesota and Patrick Kennedy from Rhode Island to introduce the Medicare Mental Health Modernization Act, a bill to provide mental health parity in Medicare. I have introduced a version of this bill in every Congress since 1994. Perhaps this time we can actually enact it.

Medicare's mental health benefit is fashioned on treatments provided in 1965, but mental health care has changed dramatically over the last 42 years. Medicare limits inpatient coverage at psychiatric hospitals to 190 days over an individual's lifetime. In addition, beneficiaries are charged a discriminatory 50 percent coinsurance for outpatient psychotherapy services, compared to 20 percent for physical health services.

The Medicare Mental Health Modernization Act eliminates this blatant mental health discrimination under Medicare and modernizes the Medicare mental health benefit to meet today's standards of care.

This bill is long overdue. One in five members of our senior population displays mental difficulties that are not part of the normal aging process. In primary care settings, more than a third of senior citizens demonstrate symptoms of depression and impaired social functioning. Yet only one out of every three mentally ill seniors receives the mental health services he/she needs. Older adults also have one of the highest rates of suicide of any segment of our population. In addition, mental illness is the single largest diagnostic category for Medicare beneficiaries who qualify as disabled . . .

The Medicare Mental Health Modernization Act is a straightforward bill that improves Medicare's mental health benefits as follows:

It reduces the discriminatory co-payment for outpatient mental health services from 50 percent to the 20 percent level charged for most other Part B medical services.

It eliminates the arbitrary 190-day lifetime cap on inpatient services in psychiatric hospitals.

It improves beneficiary access to mental health services by including within Medicare a number of community-based residential and intensive outpatient mental health services that characterize today's state-of-the-art clinical practices.

It further improves access to needed mental health services by addressing the shortage of qualified mental health professionals serving older and disabled Americans in rural and other medically underserved areas by allowing state licensed marriage and family therapists and mental health counselors to provide Medicare-covered services.

Similarly, it corrects a legislative oversight that will facilitate the provision of mental health services by clinical social workers within skilled nursing facilities.[2]

3.3   FORMAT YOUR PAPER AND ITS CONTENTS PROFESSIONALLY

Your format makes your paper's first impression. Justly or not, accurately or not, it announces your professional competence—or lack of competence. A well-executed format implies that your paper is worth reading. More importantly, however, a proper format brings information to your readers in a familiar form that has the effect of setting their minds at ease. Your paper's format should therefore impress your readers with your academic competence as a psychologist by following accepted professional standards. Like the style and clarity of your writing, your format communicates messages that are often more readily and profoundly received than the content of the document itself.

The formats described in this chapter conform with generally accepted standards in the discipline of psychology, including instructions for the following elements:

General page formats

Title page

Abstract

Text

Outline page

Table of contents

Reference page

List of tables and figures

Appendices

---

[2]   Stark, F. Introducing the Medicare Mental Health Modernization Act (extensions of remarks—March 23, 2007). 110th Cong., 1st Sess., 153 Cong. Rec. 72 (2007).

Except for special instructions from your instructor, follow the directions in this manual exactly.

General Page Formats

Psychology assignments should be printed on 8.5-by-11-inch premium white bond paper, 20 pound or heavier. Do not use any other size or color except to comply with special instructions from your instructor, and do not use off-white or poor quality (draft) paper. Psychology that is worth the time to write and read is worth good paper.

Always submit to your instructor an original typed or computer-printed manuscript. Do not submit a photocopy! Always make a second paper copy and back up your electronic copy for your own files in case the original is lost.

Margins, except in theses and dissertations, should be one inch on all sides of the paper. Unless otherwise instructed, all pages should be double-spaced in a 12-point word-processing font or typewriter pica type. Typewriter elite type may be used if another is not available. Select a font that is plain and easy to read, such as Helvetica, Courier, Garamond, or Times New Roman, which is the typeface preferred for work submitted for publication to the American Psychological Association. Do not use script, stylized, or elaborate fonts.

Page numbers should appear in the upper right-hand corner of each page, starting immediately after the title page. No page number should appear on the title page or on the first page of the text. Page numbers should appear one inch from the right side and one-half inch from the top of the page. They should proceed consecutively beginning with the title page (although the first number is not actually printed on the title page). You may use lowercase roman numerals (i, ii, iii, iv, v, vi, vii, viii, ix, x, and so on) for the title page, table of contents, table of figures, and other pages that precede the first page of text, but if you use them, the numbers must be placed at the center of the bottom of the page. Do not type in page numbers yourself; rather, use your word processor's automatic page numbering program.

Ask your instructor about bindings. In the absence of further directions, do not bind your paper or enclose it within a plastic cover sheet. Place one staple in the upper left-hand corner, or use a paper clip at the top of the paper. Note that a paper to be submitted to a journal for publication should not be clipped, stapled, or bound in any form.

Title Page

The following information will be centered on the title page:

Title of the paper
Name of writer
Course name, section number, and instructor
College or university
Date

Emotional Intelligence and High School Culture

by

Nicole Ashley Linscheid

Emotions and Intelligence

PSY313

Dr. Fred Raznick

Sage University

January 30, 2017

As the sample title page above shows, the title should clearly describe the problem addressed in the paper. If the paper discusses bullying behavior in adolescent males, for example, the title "Bullying Behavior in Adolescent Males" is professional, clear, and helpful to the reader. Titles such as "Bullying Behavior" and "Adolescent Males" are too vague to be effective. Also, the title should not be "cute." A cute title may attract attention for a play on Broadway, but it will detract from the credibility of a paper in psychology. "Bullying Behavior in Adolescent Males" is professional. "Big Bad Bully" is not.

Abstract

An abstract is a brief summary of a paper written primarily to allow potential readers to see if the paper contains information of sufficient interest for them to read. People conducting research want specific kinds of information, and they often read dozens of abstracts looking for papers that contain relevant data. Abstracts have the designation "Abstract" centered near the top of the page. Next is the title, also centered, followed by a paragraph that precisely states the paper's topic, research and analysis methods, and results and conclusions. The abstract should be written in one paragraph of no more than 150 to 250 words. Remember, an abstract is not an introduction; instead, it is a summary, as demonstrated in the sample below of an abstract from an actual published article:

Abstract

Sense-Making under Ignorance

Much of cognition allows us to make sense of things by explaining observable evidence in terms of unobservable explanations, such as category memberships and hidden causes. Yet we must often make such explanatory inferences with incomplete evidence, where we are ignorant about some relevant facts or diagnostic features. In seven experiments, we studied how people make explanatory inferences under these uncertain conditions, testing the possibility that people attempt to *infer* the presence or absence of diagnostic evidence on the basis of other cues such as evidence base rates (even when these cues are normatively irrelevant) and then proceed to make explanatory inferences on the basis of the inferred evidence. Participants followed this strategy in both diagnostic causal reasoning (Experiments 1–4, 7) and in categorization (Experiments 5–6), leading to illusory inferences. Two processing predictions of this account were also confirmed, concerning participants' evidence-seeking behavior (Experiment 4) and their beliefs about the likely presence or absence of the evidence (Experiment 5). These findings reveal deep commonalities between superficially distinct forms of diagnostic reasoning—causal reasoning and classification—and point toward common inferential machinery across explanatory tasks.[3]

Outline

See section 2.2 of this manual for information on how to structure an effective outline.

Table of Contents

A table of contents does not provide as much information as an outline, but it does include the titles of the major divisions and subdivisions of a paper. Tables of contents are not normally required in student papers or papers presented at professional meetings, but they may be included. They are normally required, however, in books, theses, and dissertations. The table of contents should consist of the chapter or main section titles, the headings used in the text, and one additional level of titles along with their page numbers, as the sample below demonstrates.

[3] Johnson, S. G., Rajeev-Kumar, G., & Keil, F. C. (2016). Sense-making under ignorance. *Cognitive Psychology, 89,* 39–70. Retrieved from doi:10.1016/j.cogpsych.2016.06.004

Text

Ask your instructor for the number of pages required for the paper you are writing. Follow the general page formats given in this chapter.

Chapter Headings

The *Publication Manual of the American Psychological Association* recommends five levels of headings:

- **Level 1**, which should be centered, in boldface, and using headline-style capitalization (the first letter of each word capitalized except for articles, prepositions, and conjunctions)
- **Level 2**, which begins at the left margin, in boldface and using headline-style capitalization, with the first line of the succeeding text beginning on the next line
- **Level 3**, which begins with an indent, uses boldface and sentence-style capitalization (only the first letter of the opening word and of proper nouns capitalized), and ends with a period, followed on the same line by the first line of the succeeding text
- **Level 4**, which is exactly like a Level 3 heading except it is italicized
- **Level 5**, which is exactly like a Level 4 heading except without boldface

The following illustration shows the proper use of chapter headings:

Impaired Cognition From a report published in the fifteenth edition of the British Association of Health Professionals (1942), the concept	(Level 1 Heading)
Impaired Cognition in Adults From a report published in the fifteenth edition of the British Association of Health Professionals (1942), the concept of lost or	(Level 2 Heading)
Impaired Cognition in Adults. From a report published in the fifteenth edition of the British Association of Health Pro-	(Level 3 Heading)
Impaired Cognition in Adults. From a report published in the fifteenth edition of the British Association of Health Pro-	(Level 4 Heading)
Impaired Cognition in Adults. From a report published in the fifteenth edition of the British Association of Health Pro-	(Level 5 Heading)

Reference Page

The format for references is discussed in detail in the source citation information that is contained in section 3.4 of this chapter.

Tables, Illustrations, Figures, and Appendices

If your paper includes tables, illustrations, or figures, include a page after the table of contents listing each of them by the name used for it in the paper's text. List the items in the order in which they appear in the paper, along with their page numbers.

You may list tables, illustrations, and figures together under the title "Figures" (and refer to them all as figures in the text), or if you have more than a half page of entries, you may have separate lists for tables, illustrations, and figures (titled accordingly in the text). An example of the format for such lists is given below.

Tables   Tables are used in the text to show relationships among data or to help the reader come to a conclusion or understand a certain point. Tables that show simple results or "raw" data should be placed in an appendix. Tables should not reiterate

TABLE 3.1

Deaths Due to Drug Overdose, 2000–2013 (per 100,000 population)

Year	New Mexico	United States
2000	15.2	6.2
2001	14.4	6.8
2002	16.3	8.2
2003	19.0	8.9
2004	16.3	9.4
2005	19.8	10.1
2006	21.4	11.5
2007	22.5	11.9
2008	26.4	11.9
2009	21.6	11.9
2010	23.3	12.3
2011	25.9	13.2
2012	24.1	13.1
2013	21.8	13.8

Note: In 2013, New Mexico had the third highest total drug overdose death rate per 100,000 population in the nation (most recent data available).
Source: Health indicator report of drug overdose deaths. (2015, November 2). *New Mexico's Indicator-Based Information System (NM-IBIS)*. Retrieved from http://ibis.health.state.nm.us

the content of the text. They should say something new, and they should stand on their own. In other words, the reader should be able to understand the table without reading the text. Clearly label the columns and rows in the table. Each word in the title (except articles, prepositions, and conjunctions) should be capitalized. The source of the information should be shown immediately below the table, not in a footnote or endnote. See Table 3.1 above.

Illustrations and Figures   Illustrations are not normally inserted in the text of a psychology paper or even in an appendix unless they are necessary to explain the content. If illustrations are necessary, do not paste or tape photocopies of photographs or similar materials to the text or the appendix. Instead, photocopy each one on a separate sheet of paper and center it, along with its typed title, within the normal margins of the paper. The format of illustration titles should be the same as that for tables and figures.

Appendices   Appendices are reference materials provided for the convenience of the reader at the back of the paper, after the text. Providing information that supplements the important facts in the text, they may include maps, charts, tables, and other selected documents. Do not place materials that are merely interesting or decorative in your appendix. Use only items that will answer questions raised by the text or are necessary to explain the text. Follow the guidelines for formats for tables, illustrations, and figures when adding material in an appendix. At the top center of the page, label your first appendix "Appendix A," your second appendix "Appendix B," and so on. Do not append an entire government report, journal article, or other publication, but only the portions of such documents that are necessary to support your paper. The source of the information should always be evident on the appended pages.

Read&Write 3.3   Explain the Data in the Table

Your task in this chapter is first to examine the data in Table 3.1, "Deaths Due to Drug Overdose, 2000–2013." Next, explain what the table tells you. What do the data mean? Then determine reasons for what the note, "In 2013, New Mexico had the third highest total drug overdose death rate per 100,000 population in the nation (most recent data available)," says. In other words, why are drug overdose deaths in New Mexico so high? Your research will take you beyond statistics into studies that attempt to identify causes for unusually high numbers of overdose deaths.

3.4   CITE YOUR SOURCES PROPERLY IN APA STYLE

One of your most important jobs as a research writer is to document your use of source material carefully and clearly. Failure to do so will cause your readers confusion, damage the effectiveness of your paper, and perhaps make you vulnerable to a charge of plagiarism. Proper documentation is more than just good form. It is a powerful indicator of your own commitment to scholarship and the sense of authority that you bring to your writing. Good documentation demonstrates your expertise as a researcher and increases your reader's trust in you and your work.

Unfortunately, as anybody who has ever written a research paper knows, getting the documentation right can be a frustrating, confusing job, especially for the novice writer. Positioning each element of a single reference citation accurately can require what seems an inordinate amount of time spent thumbing through the style manual. Even before you begin to work on specific citations, there are important questions of style and format to answer.

What to Document

Direct quotes must always be credited, as must certain kinds of paraphrased material. Information that is basic—important dates, and facts or opinions universally acknowledged—need not be cited. Information that is not widely known, whether fact or opinion, should receive documentation.

What if you are unsure whether a certain fact is widely known? You are, after all, very probably a newcomer to the field in which you are conducting your research. If in doubt, supply the documentation. It is better to overdocument than to fail to do justice to a source.

The Choice of Style

While in some classes the instructor may tell you which documentation style to use, other instructors may allow you a choice. The most widely accepted style in the discipline of psychology is that of the American Psychological Association (APA), published in the sixth edition of the *Publication Manual of the American Psychological Association* (2010). Read through the following pages before trying to use them to structure your notes. Student researchers often tend to ignore the documentation section of their style manual until the moment the first note has to be worked out, and then they skim through the examples looking for the one that perfectly corresponds to the immediate case in hand. But most style manuals do not include every possible documentation model, so the writer must piece together a coherent reference out of elements from several models. Reading through all the models before using them gives you a feel for where to find different aspects of models as well as for how the referencing system works in general.

The APA style uses an author-date system of referencing, also known as a parenthetical-reference system. Such a system requires two components for each significant reference to a source: (1) a note placed within the text, in parentheses, near where the source material occurs and (2) a full bibliographical reference for the source, placed in a list of references following the text and keyed to the parenthetical reference within the text. Models for both parenthetical notes and full references are given in the following section.

Samples of Text Citations in APA Citation Style

One Work by One Author To cite both the author's name and the year of publication in the text, use this format:

. . . was challenged by Lewissohn in 2015

Here is an author's name in the text with the year of publication in parentheses:

Freedman (2016) postulates that when individuals . . .

If you want both the author's name and the year of publication in parentheses, use this model:

. . . encouraged more aggressive play (Perrez, 2014) and contribute . . .

When the citation appears at the end of a sentence, the parenthetical reference is placed inside the period:

. . . and avoid the problem (Keaster, 2016).

In all cases, use only the author's surname, and do not include suffixes such as *Jr.*

One Work by Two, Three, Four, or Five Authors   Every time a reference to a work with two authors occurs in your text, include the surnames of both authors in your citation. For works with three, four, or five authors, cite surnames for all authors in your first text citation, and in all subsequent citations include only the surname of the first author, followed by the phrase "et al.," in roman type and followed by a period. End with the year if it is the first citation of the reference within the paragraph:

. . . however, according to Holmes and Bacon (2017), the victim never establishes a sense of self

. . . establishes a sense of self (Holmes & Bacon, 2017)

. . . found the requirements very restrictive (Mollar, Querley, & McLarry, 1926)

. . . proved to be quite difficult (Mollar et al., 1926)

. . . according to Mollar et al. (1926) . . .

Note: For all sources with more than one author, separate the last two names with the word *and* if they are given within the text and by an ampersand if they appear within parentheses.

One Work by Six or More Authors   In all references to sources with six or more authors, cite only the surname of the first author, followed by a comma and the phrase "et al.," in roman type, followed by a period and the date:

Kineson, et al. (1933) made the following suggestion . . .

When references to two multiple-author sources with the same year shorten to the same abbreviated format, cite as many of the authors as needed to differentiate the sources. Consider these examples:

Keeler, Allen, Pike, Johnson, and Keaton (2014)

Keeler, Allen, Schmidt, Wendelson, Crawford, and Blaine (2014)

Using the standard method for abbreviating citations, these two sources would both shorten to the same format:

Keeler, et al. (2014)

However, to avoid confusion, shorten the citations to these works as follows:

Keeler, Allen, Pike, et al. (2014)

Keeler, Allen, Schmidt, et al. (2014)

Group as Author Use the complete name of a group author in the first citation:

. . . to raise the standard of living (National Association of Food Retailers, 2010)

If the name of the group is lengthy, and if its abbreviation is easily identified by the general public, you may abbreviate the group name in citations after the first one.

First citation:

. . . usually kept in cages (Society for the Prevention of Cruelty to Animals, 2017)

Subsequent citations:

. . . which, according to the SPCA (2017), . . .

Remember that you must be sure to give enough information in the text citation to point the reader clearly to the full entry in the reference list.

Authors with Same Surname Use initials to differentiate authors with the same last name, even if the dates of publication are different:

. . . the new sentencing laws (K. Grady, 1999)

. . . to reduce recidivism (B. Grady, 2017)

Two Works by Same Author If the two citations appear in the same note, place a comma between the publication dates:

George (2012, 2013) argues for . . .

If the two works were published in the same year, differentiate them by adding lowercase letters as suffixes to the publication dates. Be sure also to add the suffixes to the entries in the list of references, where you will assign suffixes to the different works alphabetically by title of work:

. . . the city government (Estrada, 1994a, 1994b)

Work with No Author Given Begin the parenthetical reference of a work by an unnamed author with the first few words of the entry from the reference list—usually the title—either italicizing them if they are part of the title of a book or placing them in quotation marks if they are part of the title of an essay, newspaper article, or chapter:

... then recovery is unlikely (*Around the Bend*, 2010)

... will evidence the same behavioral problems ("Problems for Smithson," 2015)

Reference to Specific Parts of a Source   Page numbers should only be included when quoting directly from a source or referring to specific passages. Use "p." or "pp." to denote page numbers:

Thomas (2005, p. 741) builds on this scenario ...

... in the years to come (Dixon, 1997, pp. 34–35)

If your focus is limited to only a chapter, you can cite the chapter. Note that you do not abbreviate the word *chapter* in text citations, and that the word is capitalized:

... despite the fact that he never discovered the right mix of therapy and pharmaceuticals (Jessup, 2003, Chapter 4)

For an electronic source that does not use page numbers but does number the article's paragraphs, denote the paragraph using the abbreviation "para.":

Cordell (2017) insists that the court bear in mind the relatives' wishes (para. 12)

If the electronic source includes neither page nor paragraph numbers but does feature headings, you may cite the heading and, following that, the number of the paragraph from which you are taking material:

... shall be liable for damages in such a case (Johnson and Rettig, 2009, FAQs section, para. 4)

Direct Quotations   Direct quotes of fewer than 40 words should be placed in the text, with quotation marks at the beginning and end. The citation should include the author, year of publication, and page number:

Prescriptions written over the time period reflect "the staff's reluctance to use this particular class of drugs with certain age groups" (Rockett & McMinn, 2016, p. 278).

If there is no page number but the paragraph is numbered, as is sometimes the case in online sources, include that number. The following example places the author name and date within the running text:

The majority of these grant submissions, according to Peterson et al. (2009), were larded "with dubious lab results" (para. 2), and should have been thrown out.

Direct quotes of 40 words or more should start on a new line as a block quotation and be double-spaced and indented approximately half an inch (about five spaces) from the left margin, just as the first line of a paragraph is indented. Indent an additional half inch the first line of any additional paragraphs within the quotation. The parenthetical reference following the block quote is placed after the final period:

During this time Sartain (1889) and his men made a discovery that, briefly summarized in the published account, has caused consternation and confusion among American penologists for over one hundred years:

> We came to a huge structure made of stone but covered in sheathing that looked to be composed of metal, and there we were accosted in an indecipherable tongue by a set of guards most fearsomely armed and exhibiting signs of extreme agitation. One, in fact, threw his spear toward us, but owing to the distance between him and us, it did no harm.
>
> It required the discharging of but a single rifle to scatter the defenders and leave us in possession of the pile, to which, alas, we could find no door nor opening of any kind, but from within which rose, faintly, the most piteous moans any of us had ever heard men make. (p. 204)

Chapters, Tables, Appendixes, and So Forth

. . . (see Table 4 of Blake, 2014, for complete information)

. . . (see Appendix B of Shelby, 2016)

Reprints Cite by the original date of publication and the date of the edition you are using:

. . . complaints from Daniels (1922/2014), who takes a different view

More Than One Source in a Reference Separate citations by a semicolon and place them in alphabetical order by author:

. . . are related (Harmatz, 2011, p. 48; Marble et al., 2012, p. 909; Powers & Erickson, 1999, p. 48; Rackley et al., 2016, p.10; Thompson & Thompson, 2001, p. 62)

Unpublished Materials If the source is scheduled for publication at a later time, use the designation "(in press)":

A study by Barle and Ford (in press) lends support . . .

Personal Communications Materials such as letters to the author, memos, emails, messages from electronic discussion groups, and telephone conversations should be cited within the text but not listed among the references. Include in the in-text note the initials and last name of the person with whom you communicated and give as exact a date as possible:

. . . explained to the author and to the review board that the work was flawed (P. L. Bingam, personal communication, February 20, 2011)

. . . agrees, for the most part, with the findings and opinions of W. E. Knight (personal communication, October 12, 2016)

Undated Materials For undated materials, use "n.d." ("no date") in place of the date:

. . . except that Fox (n.d.) disagrees

. . . cannot be ascertained (Fox, n.d.)

Classical and Historical Texts Refer to classical and historical texts, such as the Bible, standard translations of ancient Greek writings, and the *Federalist Papers*, by using the systems by which they are subdivided, rather than the publication information of the edition you are using. Since all editions of such texts employ standard subdivisions, this reference method has the advantage of allowing your readers to find the cited passage in any published version. You may cite a biblical passage by referring to the particular book, chapter, and verse, all in roman type, with the translation (version) given after the verse number:

> "But the path of the just is as the shining light, that shineth more and more unto the perfect day" (Prov. 4:18, King James Version)

The *Federalist Papers* may be cited by their standard numbers:

> Madison addresses the problem of factions in a republic (*Federalist* 10)

If you are citing a work whose date is not known or is inapplicable, cite the year of the translation, preceded by the abbreviation "trans.," or the year of the version, followed by the word "version":

> Plato (trans. 1908) records that . . .

> . . . disagrees with the formulation in Aristotle (1892 version)

Public Documents "Appendix A7.02" in the sixth edition of the *Publication Manual of the APA* (2010) notes that text citations for legal documents are formed in the same way as text citations for other types of documents.

Legislative Hearings Information concerning a hearing before a legislative subcommittee is published in an official pamphlet. A text citation for such a pamphlet begins with a shortened form of the pamphlet's title and includes the year in which the hearing was held:

> . . . citing many of the dangers of underfunded school programs (*Funding for Inner City Schools*, 1990)

Bills and Resolutions Both enacted and unenacted bills and resolutions are cited by their number and house of origin—Senate (S.) or House of Representatives (H.R.)—and year. For example, the parenthetical reference to Unenacted Bill Number 7658, originating in the Senate in 1996, would be handled in one of the following ways:

> . . . cannot reject visa requests out of hand (S. 7658, 1996)

> . . . cannot reject visa requests out of hand (Senate Bill 7658, 1996)

> . . . according to Senate Bill 7658 (1996)

A parenthetical reference to enacted resolution 94, which originated in the House of Representatives in 1993, would read as follows:

> . . . only to U.S. citizens (H.R. Res. 94, 1993)

> House Resolution 94 (1993) explains that . . .

Statutes in Federal Code In the text, cite the popular or official name of the act and the year:

. . . in order to obtain a therapist's license (Mental Health Act of 2015)

. . . as provided by the Mental Health Act of 2015, . . .

Federal Reports   The text and parenthetical references, respectively, to a report from the Senate or House of Representatives are handled as follows:

. . . as was finally explained in Senate Report No. 85 (1989), the . . .

. . . was finally clarified (H.R. Rep. No. 114, 2009)

Court Decisions

. . . which she failed to meet (*State of Nevada v. Goldie Warren*, 1969)

. . . as was ruled in State of Nevada v. Goldie Warren (1969)

Executive Orders

Executive Order No. 13,521 (1993) states that . . .

It was clearly decided (Executive Order No. 13,521, 1993) that . . .

References in APA Style

Parenthetical citations in the text point the reader to the fuller source descriptions at the end of the paper, known as the reference list or bibliography. According to the sixth edition of the *Publication Manual of the APA* (2010, p. 180, n. 1), there is a difference between a reference list and a bibliography of sources consulted for a paper. A reference list gives only those sources used directly in the paper for support, whereas a bibliography may also include materials used indirectly, perhaps for background or further reading—materials, in other words, that do not appear directly in the paper, either in actual quotations or in paraphrase. Ask your instructor which type of source list you should provide for your class paper.

Like all other parts of the paper, the reference list should be double-spaced. Entries are alphabetized by the first element in each citation. (See the sample reference page at the end of this chapter.) The APA reference system uses "sentence-style" capitalization for titles of books and articles, meaning that only the first word of the title and subtitle (if present) and all proper names are capitalized. Titles of periodicals, including journals and newspapers, are given standard, or "headline style," capitalization. In this style all words in a title, except articles (*a, an, the*), coordinating words (*and, but, or, for, nor*), and prepositions (*among, by, for, of, to, toward*), are capitalized. Although the titles of journals and books are italicized, titles of chapters or articles are neither italicized or underlined nor enclosed in quotation marks.

These capitalization and italicizing rules mean that your reproduction of the titles of works you cite in your reference list will very probably not look like they do in the original document. For example, while a book title may appear in all capital letters on the book's title page—STRESS IN THE AMERICAN WORKPLACE—in an APA-style reference page it will conform to APA format rules: *Stress in the American workplace.*

As with most alphabetically arranged bibliographies, there is a kind of reverse-indentation system, commonly called a *hanging indent*: after the first line of a citation, which is set flush left, all subsequent lines are indented five spaces. Certain word-processing programs such as Microsoft Word offer a command that will apply hanging indent format to blocks of material.

> **Note:** If there is only one reference in your list, title the section "Reference" instead of "References." Capitalize only the first letter of the word.

Samples of APA Reference Style

Books

One Author   For a single-author source, the author's last name comes first, then the initials of the first and, if available, middle names. Add a space after each initial. The date of publication follows in parentheses, followed by a period and then the title of the book, in italics. The city of publication is cited next, then the state or territory, using U.S. postal abbreviations. If the location is outside the United States, spell out the names of the city and country. The name of the publisher is given last and in as brief a form as possible while still clear. In other words, avoid such unnecessary terms as *Publishers, and Sons, Limited, Co.,* and *Inc.*:

> Northrup, A. K. (2013). *Creative tensions in family units: Studies in be-*
> *havior.* Cleveland, OH: Johnstown.

Periods divide most of the elements in the citation, although a colon is used between the place of publication and publisher. Custom dictates that the main title of a book and its subtitle are separated by a colon, even though a colon may not appear in the title as printed on the title page of the book. Capitalize the first word of the subtitle.

Two Authors   Reverse both names, placing a comma after the initials of the first name. Separate the names by an ampersand:

> Spence, M. L., & Ruel, K. M. (2017). *Therapy, illness, and the law.* London,
> England: Tildale.

Three or More Authors   List the names and initials, in reversed order, of all authors of a source if there are six or fewer authors. If there are more than six authors, place the phrase "et al."—in roman type and with a period after "al"— following the name of the sixth author, and do not list the remaining names of authors.

> Moore, J. B., Macrory, K. L., Rice, A. D., Traylor, N. P., Wallo, B., Denison,
> W. L., et al. (2006). *Violence against women in the workplace: An*
> *overview.* Norman: University of Oklahoma Press.

As this model indicates, if the publisher is a university with the name of the state or province in its title, do not repeat that name in the location preceding the colon.

Multiple-author entries with the same first author should be alphabetized in the list of references by the surname of the second author. If the second author is the same also, then alphabetize by the surname of the third author, and so on.

Group as Author   Alphabetize such entries according to the first significant word in the group's name, and spell out the name completely:

National Association of Physical Therapists. (2017). *Standardization of physical therapy techniques.* Trenton, NJ: Arkway.

Work with No Author Given   Begin the citation with the title of the work, alphabetizing according to the first significant word:

Around the bend: Physical and emotional distress among civic administrators. (2010). Dallas, TX: Turbo.

Editor or Compiler as Author

Jastow, X. R. (Comp.). (2016). *Saying good-bye: Pathologies in Soviet literature.* New York, NY: Broadus.

Yarrow, P. T., & Edgarton, S. P. (Eds.). (1987). The *Waco protocol and the prevention of violence.* New York, NY: Halley.

Book with Author and Editor   When a book has both an author and an editor, there is no comma between the title and the parentheses enclosing the editor's name, and the editor's last name and initials are not reversed:

Scarborough, D. L. (2014). *Written on the wind: Prison maxims* (E. K. Lightstraw, Ed.). Beaufort, SC: Juvenal.

Translated Book   Do not reverse the last name and initials of the translator:

Zapata, E. M. (2008). *Beneath the wheel: Mental health of the prison population in Northern Mexico* (A. M. Muro, Trans.). El Paso, TX: Del Norte.

Untranslated Book   Provide a translation of the title, in brackets, following the title:

Wharton, E. N. (1916). *Voyages au front* [Visits to the front]. Paris, France: Plon.

Two Works by Same Author   Do not use a rule in place of the author's name in the second and subsequent entries; always state the author's name in full and give the earlier reference first:

George, J. B. (2012). *Who shot John: Psychological profiles of gunshot victims in the Midwest, 1950–1955.* Okarche, OK: Flench & Stratton.

George, J. B. (2017). *They often said so: Repetition and obfuscation in nineteenth-century psychotherapy.* Stroud, OK: Casten.

If both works by the same author were published in the same year, order the entries in your reference list alphabetically by title, excluding *A, An,* or *The.*

Author of Foreword or Introduction   List the entry under the name of the author of the foreword or introduction, not the author of the book:

Farris, C. J. (2010). Foreword. In B. Givan, *Sex crimes among the professoriat: A case study* (pp. 1–24). New York, NY: Galapagos.

Selection in Multiauthor Collection

Gray, A. N. (1998). Foreign policy and the foreign press. In B. Bonnard & L. F. Guinness (Eds.), *Current psychotherapy issues* (pp. 188–204). New York, NY: Boulanger.

You must provide a complete citation for every selection from a multiauthor collection that appears in the references; do not abbreviate the name of the collection, even if it is included as a separate entry in the reference list.

Signed Article in a Reference Book

Jenks, S. P. (1983). Fuller, Buckminster. In L. B. Sherman & B. H. Sherman (Eds.), *International dictionary of psychology* (pp. 204–205). Boston, MA: R. R. Hemphill.

Unsigned Article in an Encyclopedia

Pathologies. (2017). In *Encyclopedia of criminals and criminology* (4th ed.). Boston, MA: Blankenship.

Subsequent Editions   If you are using an edition of a book other than the first, you must cite the number of the edition or the status (such as *Rev. ed.* for revised edition) if there is no edition number:

Hales, S. A. (2010). *The water wars* (3d ed.). Pittsburgh, PA: Blue Skies.

Peters, D. K. (1972). *Social conditioning in early childhood* (Rev. ed.). Riverside, CA: Ingot.

Republished Book

Hollander, W. A. (2013). Causes of aggressive behavior in minority populations. In Y. Dearinger & J. Bowie (Eds.), *The published works of Walter Hollander* (Vol. 2, pp. 12–298). Tulsa, OK: Leesh. (Original work published 1952)

Note that there is no period at the end of the final parentheses.

Multivolume Work   If you are citing a multivolume work in its entirety, use the following format:

Graybosch, C. S. (1988). *The rise of the unions* (Vols. 1–3). New York, NY: Starkfield.

If you are citing only one volume in a multivolume work, and that volume has its own title, use the following format:

Graybosch, C. S. (1988). *The rise of the union: Vol. 1. Bloody beginnings.* New York, NY: Starkfield.

If the volume you use within the multivolume work does not have its own title, place the volume number in parentheses:

> Bradford, C. (2006). Foucault and punishment. In P. Bishop & L. Gortch (Eds.), *French theories of rehabilitation* (Vol. 2, pp. 231–270). Austin, TX: Wolverine.

Classical Texts   According to section 6.18 of the sixth edition of the *Publication Manual of the APA* (2010), references to classical texts such as sacred books and ancient Greek verse and drama are usually confined to the text and not given citations in the list of references.

Periodicals

Journal Article   While the name of the article appears in sentence-style capitalization, the name of the journal is capitalized in standard, or headline, style and italicized. The volume number is also italicized, separated from the name of the journal by a comma and, in journals with continuous pagination (see the following text), followed by a comma. Do not use "p." or "pp." to introduce the page numbers, which are not italicized.

Journal with Continuous Pagination   Most print journals are paginated so that each issue of a volume continues the page numbering of the previous issue. The reason for such pagination is that most print journals are bound in libraries as complete volumes of several issues, and continuous pagination makes it easier to consult these large compilations. References for journals with continuous pagination do not need to include the issue number after the volume number:

> Hunzecker, J., & Roethke, T. (2012). Reaching the revived: Rehab programs in rural communities. *Review of Recidivism, 4,* 250–262.

Journal in Which Each Issue Is Paginated Separately   The issue number appears in parentheses immediately following the volume number. There is no space between the volume number and the parentheses. Unlike the volume number, which is in italics, the issue number and parentheses are in roman type. In the citation that follows, the quotation marks are necessary only because the title includes a quoted slogan:

> Skylock, B. L. (1991). "Fifty-four forty or fight!": Aggression sloganized in early America. *American History Digest, 28*(3), 25–34.

Non-English Journal Article   When using the original version of an article written in a language other than English, cite the original article, inserting a translation of the title, in brackets, after the original title:

> Kern, W. (1938). Waar verzamelde Pigafetta sijn Maleise woorden? [Where did Pigafetta collect his Malaysian words?]. *Tijdschrift voor Indische taal-, land- en volkenkunde, 78,* 191–200.

English Translation of a Journal Article   If the English translation of a non-English article is cited, give the English title without brackets:

Sczaflarski, R. (2001). The trumpeter in the tower: Solidarity and legend. *World Psychological Review, 32,* 79–95.

Magazines and Newspapers

Magazines and Newspapers Magazines, which are usually published weekly, bimonthly, or monthly, appeal to the popular audience and generally have a wider circulation than journals. *Newsweek* and *Scientific American* are examples of magazines.

Article in Monthly Magazine

Stapleton, B., & Peters, E. L. (2015, April). How it was: In the lab with Og Mandino. *Lifetime Magazine, 131*(2), 24–23, 57–59.

Article in Weekly or Bimonthly Magazine

Bruck, C. (2008, October 18). Protocol guidelines: A change in sight? *Behavior Weekly, 73,* 12–15.

Newspaper Article Notice that, unlike in journal or magazine citations, page numbers for references to newspapers are preceded by "p." or "pp."

Newspaper Article with No Author Named

Little left to do before hearing, says psychologist. (2017, January 16). *The Vernon Times,* p. A7.

Newspaper Article with Discontinuous Pages Give all the page numbers, separating them with commas:

Everett, S. (1996, February 16). An entire state of illegal aliens: How Oklahomans view their "Sooner" past. *The Carrollton Tribune,* pp. D1, D4, D7–8.

Public Documents

"Appendix 7.1: References to Legal Materials," in the sixth edition of the *Publication Manual of the APA* (2010), gives models for citations of such public documents as court decisions, statutes, and other legislative and executive materials, but it also points authors to the 18th edition of *The Bluebook: A Uniform System of Citation* (2005) for more detailed instructions on how to cite such documents. Here are models for some sources frequently used by, for example, criminal justice professionals.

Legislative Hearings Information concerning a hearing before a legislative subcommittee is published in an official pamphlet, which is cited as follows:

Funding for intelligence testing: Hearing before the Subcommittee on Education Reform of the Education Committee, House of Representatives, 103d Cong., 2d Sess. 1 (1993).

This citation refers to the official pamphlet reporting on the hearing named, which was held in the U.S. House of Representatives during the second session of the 103d Congress. The report of the hearing begins on page 1 of the pamphlet.

Bills and Resolutions   Bills and resolutions are cited by their number, house of origin—Senate (S.) or House of Representatives (H.R.)—and year.

Unenacted Federal Bills and Resolutions   The following citation refers to Unenacted Bill Number 2010 from the U.S. Senate:

Better Pharmaceuticals for Children Act, S. 2010, 103d Cong. (1993).

Enacted Federal Bills and Resolutions   The following citation refers to House Resolution number 192, reported on page 4281 of volume 152 of the *Congressional Record*:

H.R. Res. 192, 104th Cong., 2d Sess. 152 Cong. Rec. 4281 (1994).

Statutes in Federal Codes   The following entry refers to an act located at section (§) 1043 of title 51 of the *United States Code Annotated*, the unofficial version of the *United States Code*:

Fish and Game Act of 1990, 51 U.S.C.A. § 1043 *et seq.* (West, 1993).

The material in parentheses indicates that the volume of the *United States Code Annotated* in which the statute is found was published in 1993 by West Publishing. The phrase *et seq.*, Latin for "and following," indicates that the act is also mentioned in later sections of the volume.

Federal Reports   The following citation refers to a report from the House of Representatives. The report number is hyphenated, the first half referring to the year of Congress (101) and the second half to the number of the report.

H. Rep. No. 101-409 (1990).

Citation for a document from the Senate would start with "S." instead of "H. Rep."

Court Decisions   While the name of the case is italicized in the text citation, it appears in roman type in the full reference.

Unpublished Cases   The following citation refers to a case filed in the U.S. Supreme Court on October 3, 1992, under docket number 46-2097:

Metrano v. Vandelay Industries, No. 46-2097 (U.S. Oct. 3, 1992).

Published Cases   The following citation refers to a case published in volume 102 of the *Federal Supplement*, beginning on page 482:

Jacob v. Warren, 102 F. Supp. 482 (W. D. Nev. 1969).

The decision in the case was rendered by the federal district court for the Western District of Nevada in 1969.

Executive Orders   Executive orders are reported in volume 3 of the *Code of Federal Regulations*. The following cites an order that appears on page 305:

Exec. Order No. 13,521, 3 C.F.R. 305 (1993).

Electronic Sources

Section 6.31 of the sixth edition of the *Publication Manual of the APA* (2010) recommends that, in general, a reference for an online source should begin with information that would be present in a reference for a fixed-media (print) source, followed by the additional information needed to allow readers to retrieve the electronic version that you have cited. Usually the additional information will include the URL (uniform resource locator) of the electronic source. The URL is in effect the address of the source on the Internet, and it must be rendered with absolute accuracy. This means that, since the URL is generally the final element in the reference, you should not place a final period at the end of a reference that includes a URL, because the period may be misinterpreted as part of the URL path. You may break a URL that wraps from one line to the next immediately before most punctuation (an exception to this rule is http://). Do not add a hyphen at the break.

The DOI System

Because of the ephemeral nature of all content on the Internet—the ease with which material is often moved, altered, or deleted—a group of international publishers is working to establish a reliable, persistent identification system for managing online content. The DOI (digital object identifier) system provides a stable method for finding Internet content by tagging such content with a unique alphanumeric string that will serve as a persistent link to the content's Internet location. The alphanumeric string, called a DOI, is assigned by a registration agency that provides linking services for publishers. The agency called CrossRef, for example, serves as a linking service for materials published by the scientific community. A reader searching for an article whose entry in a reference list includes a DOI can enter that DOI into the *DOI resolver* search field provided by CrossRef.org and be directed to the article, or else to a link for purchasing it.

A DOI can be attached to print as well as electronic material; when a book or an article has been assigned a DOI, that string can be made part of a reference entry, and no further retrieval information is necessary to identify and locate the material. This means that if you include the DOI in your reference, you need not also include the source's URL. The referencing system presented in the sixth edition of the *Publication Manual of the APA* (2010) provides models for references using the DOI system. Examples of such models follow.

A DOI string usually begins with a "10," followed by a prefix of four or more digits that identifies the organization that has established the DOI for the content. A slash separates the prefix from a suffix, a list of alphanumeric digits, often quite long, determined by the publisher. A DOI typically looks like this:

doi:10.1008/ambi.2119.0568

The four-digit string following the first period—"1008"—is the prefix; the material following the slash is the suffix. Notice that the "doi" is not capitalized.

If a DOI has been assigned to an electronic text—an electronic journal article, for example—the string can usually be found on the text's first page near the copyright notice, as well as on the database landing page for the article. It is important to reproduce the DOI in your reference exactly. Do not place a period after the DOI in the reference, since the period may be misinterpreted as part of the DOI.

Here are models for several of the kinds of references commonly required in criminal justice research work.

Electronic Books

Electronic Version of Print Book   It is unnecessary to include the name and place of the publisher, even if there is a print version of the book.

Moore, J. B., Macrory, K. L., Rice, A. D., Traylor, N. P., Wallo, B., Denison, W. L., et al. (2006). *Violence against women in the workplace: An overview*. Retrieved from http://www.crjus.org/lectronic/fb99/indata.html

With editor as author:

Barton, P. L. (Ed.). (2009). *Sex offenders and residency laws*. Retrieved from https://www .aacjdir.org/reports/survey-205/publications/jinx.htm

Electronic-Only Book

Marshal, S. (n.d.). *The small-town counselor: Myths and realities*. Retrieved from https://www.hillsboro.com/texark.asp?itemPP=20

Electronic Version of Republished Book

Hollander, W. A. (2013). Causes of aggressive behavior in minority populations. In Y. Dearinger & J. Bowie (Eds.), *The published works of Walter Hollander* (Vol. 2, pp. 12–298). Retrieved from https://www.skinnerset .saunders.com (Original work published 1952)

Book with DOI

Alexander, S. (2016). *Mental health in rural Tennessee*. doi:10.4211/07666642

Selection in a Multiauthor Collection

Chapman, E. T., & Snadon, V. L. (2000). Criminal behavior management in a post-9/11 world. In J. Darl, L. Palm, & R. Palm (Eds.), *The new age of therapy* (pp. 220–251). Retrieved from http://www.okresdef.org/anthol /smithson.html

Unsigned Article in a Reference Work

Inevitable discovery rule. (1999). In P. Thomas (Ed.), *Encyclopedia of psychotherapy* (4th ed., Vol. 2). Retrieved from https://www.fabenslaw .com/horizondate-71/white.html

Electronic Periodicals   Section 6.32 of the sixth edition of the *Publication Manual of the APA* (2010) explains that it is generally unnecessary to include database information in references, since the content coverage of most databases changes over time. For the same reason, it is not necessary to include information identifying such database aggregators as EBSCO, OVID, and ProQuest.

Volume numbers, issue numbers, and page numbers are often not provided for an online source, but if they are, be sure to include them.

Journal Article   If the article is an exact duplicate of a print version, as in a PDF version, give the inclusive page numbers:

> Capulet, T. J., & Finster, R. T. Licensed therapists as municipal problem solvers. *Community Health Review*, 4(2), 24–41. Retrieved from https://www.goldstar.lib.edu

Journal Article with DOI

> Lissette, A. N., & Kingsley, W. P. (2008). Volunteer support for residential watch programs. *City Law and Country Law*, *14*, 193–212. doi:10.2148/ffssp.29.134 .22677

Online Newsletter Article

> Cordell, T. P. (2017, October). Battered children and the mental health system in Texas. *Social Justice Online*. Retrieved from http://www.social/cj.net /newslettr_topic.html

Online Newspaper Article

> Squires, A. (2005, November 12). Hard times for case workers, says mayor. *El Paso Sun Times*. Retrieved from http://www.elpasosun.com/2005 -12/12.html

Message Posted to a Newsgroup, Online Forum, or Discussion Group   Provide the message subject line, or thread, after the exact date. Place any message identifier, if there is one, in brackets after the message subject line:

> Macbeth, C. (2013, April 23). Re: Boomer diagnoses get serious attention [online forum content]. Retrieved from news.cybertherapies.net /agecase.htm

Message Posted to an Electronic Mailing List

> Barnes, P. (2010, January 14). Re: Death toll in drug war [Electronic mailing list message]. Retrieved from http://westex.elmclub/stats /message12

CD-ROM Source

> Gower, B., & Bensonhurst, P. B. (2001). Reclaiming inner-city environments: The role of the church [CD-ROM]. Humanities Omnibus.

Personal Communications, Print and Electronic   According to section 6.20 of the sixth edition of the *Publication Manual of the APA* (2010), personal communications such as letters, memos, and telephone and email messages are cited within the text but do not appear in the reference list since the data they provide are not recoverable.

A sample reference page follows.

References

Alexander, S. (2016). *Mental health in rural Tennessee*. doi:10.4211/07666642

Barnes, P. (2010, January 14). Re: Death toll in drug war [Electronic mailing list message]. Retrieved from http://westex.elmclub/stats/message12/terminal

Cordell, T. P. (2017, October). Battered children and the mental health system in Texas. *Social Justice Online*. Retrieved from http://www.social/cj.net /newslettr_topic.html

Everett, S. (1996, February 16). An entire state of illegal aliens: How Oklahomans view their "Sooner" past. *The Carrollton Tribune*, pp. D1, D4, D7–8.

Hollander, W. A. (2013). Causes of aggressive behavior in minority populations. In Y. Dearinger & J. Bowie (Eds.), *The published works of Walter Hollander* (Vol. 2, pp. 12–298). Tulsa, OK: Leesh. (Original work published 1952)

Hunzecker, J., & Roethke, T. (2012). Reaching the revived: Rehab programs in rural communities. *Review of Recidivism, 4*, 250–262.

Marshal, S. (n.d.). *The small-town counselor: Myths and realities*. Retrieved from https:// www .hillsboro.com/texark.asp?itemPP=20

Yarrow, P. T., & Edgarton, S. P. (Eds.). (1987). *The Waco protocol and the prevention of violence*. New York, NY: Halley.

Read & Write 3.4   Compile a Usable Bibliography

Select a topic of your choice and construct a bibliography of published sources in APA style, including ten different types of sources (journal articles, books, book reviews, online sources, etc.).

3.5   AVOID PLAGIARISM

Plagiarism is the use of someone else's words or ideas without proper credit. Although some plagiarism is deliberate, produced by writers who understand that they are guilty of a kind of academic thievery, much of it is unconscious, committed by writers who are not aware of the varieties of plagiarism or who are careless in recording their borrowings from sources. Plagiarism includes:

- Quoting directly without acknowledging the source
- Paraphrasing without acknowledging the source
- Constructing a paraphrase that closely resembles the original in language and syntax

You want to use your source material as effectively as possible. This will sometimes mean that you should quote from a source directly, whereas at other times you will want to express such information in your own words. At all times, you should work to integrate the source material skillfully into the flow of your written argument.

When to Quote

You should quote directly from a source when the original language is distinctive enough to enhance your argument, or when rewording the passage would lessen its impact. In the interest of fairness, you should also quote a passage to which you will take exception. Rarely, however, should you quote a source at great length (longer than two or three paragraphs). Nor should your paper, or any substantial section of it, be merely a string of quoted passages. The more language you take from the writings of others, the more the quotations will disrupt the rhetorical flow of your own words. Too much quoting creates a choppy patchwork of varying styles and borrowed purposes in which your sense of your own control over your material is lost.

Quotations in Relation to Your Writing

When you do use a quotation, make sure that you insert it skillfully. According to the sixth edition of the *Publication Manual of the APA* (2010), quotations of fewer than 40 words should generally be integrated into the text and set off with quotation marks:

> "In the last analysis," Mary Lewis argued in 2016, "we cannot afford not to embark on a radical program of treatment reform" (p. 12).

A quotation of 40 words or longer should be formatted as a *block quotation*; it should begin on a new line, be indented in its entirety from the left margin, and not be enclosed in quotation marks.

> Llewellyn's outlook for the solution to the problem of the nation's over-supply of qualified research scientists is anything but optimistic:
> If the trend in grantsssing graduate degrees in research psychology continues, the cost of doing nothing may be too high. Most good positions in research psychology are tenure-track university posts. Funding declines and elevated college costs have forced cutbacks in new jobs across the country. The three-year period from 2012 to 2015 shows an annual increase in under-employed researchers of roughly twenty percent. Such an upward trend for a sustained period of time would eventually reduce the supply of well qualified scientists. And yet the profession seems unable to temporarily reduce the supply of graduates. (2016, p. 8)

Acknowledge Quotations Carefully

Failing to signal the presence of a quotation skillfully can lead to confusion or choppiness:

> The President of the American Psychological Association (APA) believes that mental health services are widely underfunded due to the recent depression's lingering effects on state budgets. "America does not realize the cost to society of failing to provide adequate mental health services to its population" (Scott, 2016, p. 11).

The first sentence in the above passage seems to suggest that the quote that follows comes from the president of the APA. Note how this revision clarifies the attribution:

> According to Courtney Scott, the President of the American Psychological Association believes that mental health services are widely underfunded due to the recent depression's lingering effects on state budgets. Summarizing the APA President's view, Scott writes, "America does not realize the cost to society of failing to provide adequate mental health services to its population" (Scott, 2016, p. 11).

The origin of each quote must be indicated within your text at the point where the quote occurs as well as in the list of works cited, which follows the text.

Quote Accurately

If your transcription of a quotation introduces careless variants of any kind, you are misrepresenting your source. Proofread your quotations very carefully, paying close attention to such surface features as spelling, capitalization, italics, and the use of numerals.

Occasionally, in order to make a quotation fit smoothly into a passage, to clarify a reference, or to delete unnecessary material, you may need to change the original wording slightly. You must, however, signal any such change to your reader. Some alterations may be noted by brackets:

> "Several times in the course of his lecture, the psychology professor said that his view [on helicopter moms] remains unchanged" (McAffrey, 2016, p. 2).

Ellipses indicate that words have been left out of a quote:

> "The last time students disagreed with one of the professor's opinions . . . was back in 2012" (Pulsifer, 2015, p. 143).

When you integrate quoted material with your own prose, it is unnecessary to begin the quote with ellipses:

> Benton raised eyebrows with his claim that "nobody in the Dean's office knows how to tie a shoe, let alone solve a problem with an incompetent professor" (Seville, 2016, p. 12).

Paraphrasing

Your writing has its own rhetorical attributes, its own rhythms and structural coherence. Inserting several quotations into one section of your paper can disrupt the patterns of your prose and diminish its effectiveness. *Paraphrasing*, or recasting source material in your own words, is one way to avoid the choppiness that can result from a series of quotations.

Remember that a paraphrase is to be written in your language; it is not to be a near-copy of the source writer's language. Merely changing a few words of the original does justice to no one's prose and frequently produces stilted passages. This sort of borrowing is actually a form of plagiarism. To fully integrate another's material into your own writing, use your own language.

Paraphrasing may actually increase your comprehension of source material, because in recasting a passage you will have to think very carefully about its meaning—more carefully, perhaps, than if you had merely copied it word for word.

Avoiding Plagiarism When Paraphrasing Paraphrases require the same sort of documentation as direct quotes. The words of a paraphrase may be yours, but the idea belongs to someone else. Failure to give that person credit, in the form of references within the text and in the bibliography, may make you vulnerable to a charge of plagiarism.

One way to guard against plagiarism is to keep careful notes of when you have directly quoted source material and when you have paraphrased—making sure that the wording of the paraphrases is yours. Be sure that all direct quotes in your final draft are properly set off from your own prose, either with quotation marks or in indented blocks.

What kind of paraphrased material must be acknowledged? Basic material that you find in several sources need not be documented by a reference. For example, it is unnecessary to cite a source for the information that Sigmund Freud proposed a widely accepted concept of mind (id, ego, and superego), because this is a commonly known fact. However, Professor Johnson's opinion, published in a recent article, that Freud's popularity was based upon his ability to publicize his ideas is not a fact, but a theory based on Johnson's research and defended by her. If you wish to use Johnson's opinion in a paraphrase, you need to credit her, as you should all judgments and claims from another source. Any information that is not widely known, whether factual or open to dispute, should be documented. This includes statistics, graphs, tables, and charts taken from sources other than your own primary research.

Read&Write 3.5 Summarize an Article from *In-Mind*

Select an article from a recent copy of *In-Mind* and summarize it properly in your own words, without plagiarizing, in approximately 500 words. Attach a copy of the article itself to your summary.

4

BECOME FAMILIAR
WITH PERSPECTIVES
IN PSYCHOLOGY

4.1   PSYCHODYNAMIC

Who are we, really?

Jesuit priest Pierre Teilhard de Chardin (1881–1955) provided a confident theological response to this existential mystery: "We are not human beings having a spiritual experience. We are spiritual beings having a human experience." The question of who we are, relevant as it is not only to our eternity but also to our temporal lives, has produced a number of profound answers. For Aristotle (384–322 BCE), we are political beings; for René Descartes (1596–1650), thinking beings; for John Locke (1632–1704), acquisitive beings; for Jean-Jacques Rousseau (1712–1778), institutionally corrupted beings; for Charles Darwin (1809–1882), evolved beings; for Karl Marx (1818–1883), equality-loving, economic beings; and for psychiatrist Sigmund Freud (1856–1939), primal-sexual beings.

Freud's contributions to psychology are monumental, a legacy not diminished by the fact that today's academic and practicing psychologists, inspired by advances in behavioral techniques and neurological studies, have largely moved beyond his theories and methods. Freud's rise to fame in Europe after World War I was largely due to his development and popularizing of the "talking cure" that we now call counseling. Posttraumatic stress disorder (PTSD), as it is currently known, was common among the survivors of World War I (1914–1918), and counseling, then as now, provided effective therapy for millions with PTSD and many other mental problems.

Freud's substantial professional legacy includes his success at helping us appreciate and employ the healing power of at least two phenomena: myth and mental mechanisms. His initial research was prompted in part by a fascination with what myth, in the classical sense of the word, tells us about who we are. Classical myth is by no means untruth; it is precisely the opposite: complete truth. Myths are metaphors for great mysteries, realities we experience but lack the mental capacities to confront directly, understand, and explain. Since before recorded time, myths have defined our selves, our habitations, and our gods. Just as we must view a solar eclipse indirectly, through instruments or with a visual shield, or risk damage to our retinas, so do our attempts at viewing God, an overwhelming experience, require us to look away and describe our experience in metaphors, always imperfect, always at least a slight distortion of reality. Thus, by affording us an indirect approach, myth funnels our personal tribulations into the flow of universal human experience, helping us grasp the unknowable. We feed our children a steady stream of myths, from Santa Claus to the Easter Bunny and from Aesop's fables to Cinderella. Not only do we mine our catalogs of literary history for myths, but we also manufacture them by the hundreds each year. Otherwise our children would never find the courage to try *Green Eggs and Ham* and would always fear to go *Where the Wild Things Are*.[1]

At the end of each day we adults yearn for asylum from our desks at General Electric, our tools at General Motors, and the trucks we drive for General Foods, and so we scan our 392 channels to watch Spider-Man—again. Just like the ancient Greeks, we cherish our myths. For the crime of divulging some of Zeus's secrets, for example, the Greek Judges of the Dead condemned Sisyphus to roll a boulder up a hill until it reached the peak and then send it rolling down the other side. But this feat was something the hapless minor god could never complete. The weight of the boulder was sufficient to make it always roll back, just before the top, and descend once more to its original position, an event that for Sisyphus was destined to eternally recur. No, we are not Sisyphus, and our boulders are not literal. Still, many of us feel akin to Sisyphus when we try to pay off our credit cards or face another inevitable Monday morning.

Another famous Greek myth featured Oedipus, a king who unknowingly married his mother after having killed his father. This sort of myth fascinated Freud because as he listened to patients' stories, he became convinced that we are motivated far more than we know by deeply primal unconscious desires. In fact, according to Freud, our psychosexual development governs our chances for vital, healthy, lives. Freud posited that our life spans are composed of five erogenous stages that, if not completed successfully, can disrupt our adult lives:

1. The *oral* stage, the first 18 months of life, begins with sucking and may shadow later life with smoke or alcohol.

2. The *anal* stage, the second 18 months, may, if uncompleted, lead to perfectionism or mental disarray.

3. The *phallic* stage, comprising the following three years, is a time when unconscious desire for mothers leads boys to fear castration by their fathers (the Oedipus Complex).

4. The *latency* stage, years 7 through 12, is a time of suppressed sexual desires.

5. The *genital* stage, lasting the remainder of life, may bring sexual fulfillment or complications.[2]

---

[1] Dr. Seuss. (1960). *Green eggs and ham*. New York, NY: Random House; Sendak, M. (1963). *Where the wild things are*. New York, NY: Harper & Row.

[2] A brief discussion of the five erogenous stages can be found in McLeod, S. (2008). Psychosexual stages. *SimplyPsychology*. Retrieved from https://www.simplypsychology.org/psychosexual.html

Freud's next theory mirrors, but does not duplicate, Plato's system of mental organization (body, spirit, mind). For Freud, physical appetites are controlled by the Id, the great subconscious. The Ego provides rationality, and the Superego supplies a conscience with its ensuing morality. In the struggle of the Ego and Superego to suppress the superior emotive power of the Id, the mind develops *defense mechanisms*, listed below with examples:

- With *displacement*, we can come home agitated by something at work and take it out on our partner.
- With *projection*, we may see in our child our own striving toward success.
- In *sublimation*, instead of confronting our gun-toting neighbor about his barking dog, we take a long, fast bicycle ride.
- In *denial*, instead of recognizing a fractured relationship, we ignore it and carry on as we normally do.
- In *repression*, we fail to remember a violent episode because its memory is too painful.[3]

Many of Freud's concepts thrive in today's popular culture and in counseling practice, especially among psychiatrists and psychoanalysts.

Read&Write 4.1 Meet Dali and Freud

Salvador Dali (1904–1989) was born in the Catalan (northeastern Spain) town of Figueres, and the home he designed in the nearby coastal town of Cadaqués is an adventure in daring simplicity, an extended expression of a man who painted fantastic images that both stretch our imaginations and help us navigate the simultaneous beauty and strangeness of life.

Dali's most famous painting, *The Persistence of Memory*, exemplifies his command of paradox, portraying both the end of life and the infinity of existence.

Intentionally apolitical, Dali made an accommodation with Fascist dictator Francisco Franco (1892–1975) that allowed him to coexist with a brutal regime and stay in his beloved Cadaqués for the length of Franco's reign (1939–1975) and afterward. It's at least arguable that no one captures the essence of Sigmund Freud better than Dali. The approaches and works of both men were more than a bit surreal. When the two met in London in 1938, the founder of the school of psychoanalytic theory's terminal cancer allowed them little time to become acquainted, but Dali's appreciation of Freud's concepts had already found expression in the surrealist artist's paintings for more than the previous decade.[4]

Your task in this exercise is to choose, so to speak, one or the other side of the same coin. Write an essay in which you *either* (1) select up to three concepts developed by Freud, then locate images of Dali's works that reflect these concepts, and explain your selections, *or* (2) select one or more of Dali's works and explain how one or more of Freud's concepts is reflected in them, and explain your interpretations.

---

[3] These and other defense mechanisms posited by Freud are discussed in McLeod, S. (2009). Defense mechanisms. *SimplyPsychology*. Retrieved from https://www.simplypsychology.org/defense-mechanisms.html

[4] For an account of the meeting between Dali and Freud, see Sonin, A. (2013, April 16). Heritage: Sigmund Freud met his greatest admirer Salvadore Dali at Primrose Hill Home. *Ham&High*. Retrieved from http://www.hamhigh.co.uk /news/heritage/heritage-sigmund-freud-met-his-greatest-admirer-salvadore-dali-at-primrose-hill-home-1-2016573

Many websites present the lives and works of Sigmund Freud and Salvador Dali, and you may want to begin your writing project by perusing them to gain a better appreciation of the achievements of these two men. Think of Freud and Dali with respect to concepts such as myth, science, surrealism, sexuality, paradox, metaphor, and other similar things that come to mind.

4.2 BEHAVIORIST

If you want to do research in psychology, or any other discipline for that matter, the question is always, *Where do you start?* As we mentioned in a previous chapter, the best place to begin is to identify a topic upon which research is needed and then proceed to supply the need. But there is another meaning to this question that psychologists and other scientists need to ask before they proceed, and this second sense goes back at least as far as Plato and Aristotle.

Plato's mentor Socrates began investigations by *deductive reasoning*—constructing a general principle and then deducing specific conclusions from it. He may, for example, have said to his students, "People are most successful at what they are suited to do best. Philosophers, therefore, who are good at knowing what is best for people, ought to manage societies." Plato's protégé Aristotle, however, used the reverse of this process, *inductive reasoning*: he began his investigations by observing behavior and other phenomena and then induced conclusions from them. Aristotle may have said, for example, "I have collected histories of 350 poleis [Greek city-states], and all of them exhibit cyclical patterns of political upheaval and stability. Therefore, Athens is likely to exhibit this same pattern."

Whereas psychoanalysts, evolutionary psychologists, and other researchers tend to proceed using deductive methods—building conceptual models and then deducing behaviors from those models—behaviorists believe that it makes more sense to use inductive methods in their work, observing patterns of behavior first, and then inducing predictive results from those models. The point of this chapter segment is to help you become familiar with the work of some behavioral scientists, work that has many psychological implications and applications.

Read & Write 4.2 Discover What TED Talks Says about Behavior

If you have not yet discovered the amazing world of TED Talks, you are about to. The structure of your task is quite simple. First, go online to http://www.ted.com and view the following three talks:

1. *Frans de Waal: Moral Behavior in Animals:* http://www.ted.com/talks/frans_de _waal_do_animals_have_morals

2. *The Surprisingly Logical Minds of Babies:* http://www.ted.com/talks/laura_schulz _the_surprisingly_logical_minds_of_babies

3. *Bob Nease: How to Trick Yourself into Good Behavior:* http://www.ted.com/watch /ted-institute/ted-ibm/bob-nease-how-to-trick-yourself-into-good-behavior

As you watch, take notes about interesting elements of each talk.

Second, watch each of the three talks a second time and identify (1) themes, methods, conclusions, and other aspects *common to* all three talks, and (2) themes, methods, conclusions, and other aspects that *distinguish* all three talks. Finally, write an essay in which you identify similarities and differences in the three approaches and draw your own conclusions about the value to human understanding of each of the three talks.

4.3 COGNITIVE

Consciousness, the phenomenon that defines the boundaries of cognition, has been a source of fascination and controversy for millennia. Its essential properties continue to be the focus of neurological and psychological research and the substance of discussions throughout the social sciences. Its scope and character are of vital concern to millions of religious people worldwide.

Perhaps our ontological categories are excessively confining, for a definitive definition of conscious still eludes us. What activities signify consciousness? Is consciousness merely the attractions that compel plants to lean toward the sun? Does it tell single-celled animals when to divide into two? How do quartz crystals know how to grow inside geodes? Are spiritual phenomena brain-manufactured chimeras, or external entities detected by our cranial neurons?

Discussions of consciousness appear in several popular contemporary controversies in which psychologists have leading roles. Among them are conversations about the existence of God and the human soul, technologically generated new challenges for medical ethics, and the opportunities and dangers inherent in artificial intelligence.

At a May 2016 panel on consciousness, sponsored by the New York Academy of Sciences, New York University researcher David Chalmers declared, "The scientific and philosophical consensus is that there is no nonphysical soul or ego, or at least no evidence for that."[5] Princeton University neuroscientist Michael Graziano maintained:

> Consciousness is a kind of con game the brain plays with itself. The brain is a computer that evolved to simulate the outside world. Among its internal models is a simulation of itself—a crude approximation of its own neurological processes. . . . The result is an illusion. Instead of neurons and synapses, we sense a ghostly presence—a self—inside the head. But it's all just data processing. The machine mistakenly thinks it has magic inside it, . . . and it calls the magic consciousness. It's not the existence of this inner voice he finds mysterious. The phenomenon to explain, . . . is why the brain, as a machine, insists it has this property that is nonphysical.[6]

Chalmers and Graziano are two voices on one side of the great divide in consciousness studies: those who believe that the brain *manufactures* its own phenomena. Theorists on the other side of the controversy believe that the brain *perceives* phenomena so far undetected by scientific instruments. A fascinating discussion of

5 Johnson, G. (2016, July 4). Consciousness: The mind messing with the mind. *New York Times*. Retrieved from http://www.nytimes.com/2016/07/05/science/what-is-consciousness.html
6 Ibid.

conscious is unfolding as scholars in the disciplines of religion and theology employ science to react to dismissive posturing with respect to other potential forms of consciousness.

In their book *The Mystical Mind*, Eugene d'Aquili and Andrew Newberg, drawing in part on their own pioneering work with SPECT (Single Photon Emission Computed Tomography) imagery of meditating subjects, present a detailed neurological analysis of the human brain at work during a prototypically *religious* activity. D'Aquili and Newberg build on their findings and related research to propose a "neurotheology" that in many ways turns the classic reductionist critique of mind and soul on its head. Rather than explaining *away* religious experiences as *epiphenomena* (secondary effects of other brain activity and, therefore, having no other causation), the authors propose that brain science provides powerful support for the "reality" and epistemological utility of spiritual phenomena.[7]

Turning from theology to emerging challenges for medical ethics, we encounter an impending exponential escalation in technology-driven moral dilemmas. In some ways, life in the second decade of the 21st century is simple. We still live our daily lives as the ancients did, easily differentiating animal, mineral, and vegetable. We are animal, our steak knives are mineral, and our cell phone cases are fossil-fuel-vegetable. Despite some elementary advances in biotechnology, like artificial limbs that respond directly to brain signals, we still easily distinguish between biology and technology. All this is about to change radically. Imagine a time in the not-so-distant future when biology and technology are so interwoven that we are unable to distinguish between the two. Blood cells will be programmed to fight disease. The limbs of our bodies will transmit electronic data. Artificial fossil-fuel human organs will provide us an endless supply of spare body parts. And these advances are only the beginning.

The preeminent prophet of this great biotech metamorphosis is computer scientist and futurologist Ray Kurzweil, whose 2006 book *The Singularity Is Near* has predicted processes already well under way.[8] The "Singularity" is the unified identity of biology and technology: biology will be technologized and technology will be biologized. A website for the book describes the Singularity as follows:

> That merging is the essence of the Singularity, an era in which our intelligence will become increasingly nonbiological and trillions of times more powerful than it is today—the dawning of a new civilization that will enable us to transcend our biological limitations and amplify our creativity. In this new world, there will be no clear distinction between human and machine, real reality and virtual reality. We will be able to assume different bodies and take on a range of personae at will. In practical terms, human aging and illness will be reversed; pollution will be stopped; world hunger and poverty will be solved. Nanotechnology will make it possible to create virtually any physical product using inexpensive information processes and will ultimately turn even death into a soluble problem.[9]

So what are some of the ethical problems that will emerge from the Singularity and other medical advances? The ethical umbrella herein is our emerging capacity to

7   d'Aquili, E., & Newberg, A. B. (1999). *The mystical mind: Probing the biology of religious experience* (p. 126). Minneapolis, MN: Fortress Press.
8   Kurzweil, R. (2005). *The singularity is near: When humans transcend biology*. New York: Viking.
9   About the book. (n.d.). *Singularity.com*. Retrieved from http://singularity.com/aboutthebook.html

redefine what it means to be human beings. Let's start with an ability to determine our children's aptitudes. An IQ is a barometer of cognition. Who of us will select what is now a normal IQ when everyone else will be creating geniuses, people who perceive and make new connections from their perceptions? Who of us will select normal physical abilities when everyone else will give birth to talented athletes? Who of us will settle for a child capable of playing a kazoo when a concert violinist is an option?

When (not if) we clone humans, will we inaugurate a new era of slavery? Captain America, after all, is a fiction soon to become reality. His story details how a normal human being was transformed into a superbeing by American scientists attempting to respond to a demon-human that was thought to be in the process of development by the Nazis during World War II.

Will medical ethics play a mediating role in this brave new world, or will irresist-ible competitive economic and political forces sweep us into heretofore unimagined modes of survival? The answer to this question may well be found in the answer to another: When, if ever, will artificial intelligence or supersede human consciousness?

Science fiction has already warned us of such horrors as AI beings replacing human beings altogether. According to Susan Schneider, professor of philoso-phy and cognitive science at the University of Connecticut and faculty member at Yale's Interdisciplinary Center for Bioethics, "This would be an unfathomable loss. Even the slightest chance that this could happen should give us reason to think carefully about AI consciousness."[10] What are the possible implications for human consciousness?

> First, a superintelligent AI may bypass consciousness altogether. In humans, con-sciousness is correlated with novel learning tasks that require concentration, and when a thought is under the spotlight of our attention, it is processed in a slow, sequential manner. Only a very small percentage of our mental processing is conscious at any given time. A superintelligence would surpass expert-level knowledge in every domain, with rapid-fire computations ranging over vast databases that could encom-pass the entire internet. It may not need the very mental faculties that are associated with conscious experience in humans. Consciousness could be outmoded.[11]

Schneider concludes, "We should regard the problem of AI consciousness as an open question."[12] And her final admonition is well worth considering:

> Of course, from an ethical standpoint, it is best to assume that a sophisticated AI may be conscious. For any mistake could wrongly influence the debate over whether they might be worthy of special ethical consideration as sentient beings. As the films *Ex Machina* and *I, Robot* illustrate, any failure to be charitable to AI may come back to haunt us, as they may treat us as we treated them.[13]

---

[10] Schneider, S. (2016, March 18). The problem of AI consciousness. [Blog post]. *KurzweilAINetwork*. Retrieved from http://www.kurzweilai.net/the-problem-of-ai-consciousness
[11] Ibid.
[12] Ibid.
[13] Ibid.

Read & Write 4.3 Explore Problems and Potentials of Artificial Intelligence

Applying the methods and formats described in previous chapters of this manual, write a research paper of 8 to 10 pages that discusses the relationship of consciousness to the development of artificial intelligence. Be sure to include among your sources no fewer than 10 scholarly articles, including at least three from the discipline of psychology.

5

BECOME FAMILIAR WITH

SKILLED OBSERVATION

5.1   SKILLED LISTENING

Though it receives less attention than speaking and writing, listening is a vital skill as well. You are studying psychology so that you may better understand life. Fewer things will amplify your understanding more than perceptive, active listening.

Listening is a function of attentiveness and responsiveness. As an attentive listener, you will absorb verbal, nonverbal, tonal, gestural, auditory, and physiological signals you would otherwise miss. Attentive listening means opening yourself to more than words. Attentive listening attunes your mental antenna to enhanced perception.

As you converse, learn to observe your listener. Notice if he twists hair in one spot of his head or if she tends to pick at her fingernails. Are her fists clenched much of the time? Does he avoid direct eye contact with you? Does she reach out to touch you at times as she is speaking? Have you ever noticed how some people use their hands and arms while talking? Hand motions while speaking vary a lot among cultural groups, so take that into account as you practice listening to the whole person. Part of skilled listening is sensing and accepting the talker's comfort zone, his or her personal space. The amount of personal space within which people feel comfortable varies with cultures. For example, you will normally find yourself provided wider personal space in Scotland than you will experience in Greece.

Attentiveness enhances responsiveness. As you take responsibility to become a skilled listener, the respect you thereby bestow on the person speaking to you models for that person effective listening skills. A good conversation takes on a life of its own, with each spoken sentiment or observation propagating fresh insight in the listener. Think about how it feels to be talking to someone who is clearly interested in what you have to say, who is working with you to create a conversation that is meaningful to both of you. In such moments, don't you feel your own mind is working at a higher pitch? Don't you find yourself thinking a bit better than you usually do? It all starts with listening: responsible, attentive, perceptive, and responsive listening.

Read&Write 5.1 Conduct a Focus Group

This exercise will provide an excellent opportunity to sharpen your listening skills while improving your group problem-solving skills at the same time. If your instructor finds it convenient, you can form a *focus group* in your psychology class. Focus groups are formed by businesses, government agencies, churches, and many other organizations to serve a variety of purposes: generate ideas; clarify problems, challenges, and opportunities; provide opportunities for participation; and understand diverse viewpoints. Normally composed of six to eight people, focus groups assemble for one or more sessions to discuss a specific topic or agenda.

Proceed with your focus group, therefore, by assembling six to eight people, seated in a circle. Your group will need to select a specific topic, something that contributes to your understanding of your current situation in life and the insights psychology can bring to it. Here are a few possible topics for a college classroom focus group, just to provide you an idea of what you might discuss:

- Challenges of academic achievement
- Unique opportunities of campus life
- Varieties of interpersonal relations on campus
- How college can help us know ourselves better
- Stress in college life

Plan your focus group session for the larger part of one class session. Select one person to be a moderator, someone who contributes to the conversation but also assures that the discussion stays on track and that everyone has a chance to contribute. The moderator will also take notes on the substance of the discussion and summarize both the main points of conclusions drawn and disparities in perceptions and approaches among members of the group during the process. Each participant should also take notes that, as precisely as possible, record things learned through attentive listening.

Leave time at the end of the focus group to have the group reflect on the experience. Examine the effectiveness of the focus group process. What was accomplished? What was left undone? How worthwhile was the endeavor? How can focus groups make valuable contributions to studies and other projects in the future?

At the very end, each student should write a summary of what he or she has learned by attentive listening. What did you learn about yourself that you didn't know before? What are your strengths as a listener? What areas will you be practicing (i.e., your weak spots) in future discussions? How has this exercise empowered you to recognize some finer aspects of communication? What do you appreciate about conversations that you discounted before? Do you value the conversational process more now?

5.2 SOCIAL BEHAVIOR

By the dawn of the twentieth century, Frederick Winslow Taylor (1856–1915) was perfecting techniques of what became known as scientific management. Preferring a job as a mechanic in a factory to attending Harvard University, Taylor first learned the requirements of factory life and then began to observe them. He carefully observed the details of industrial work. How many steps did a worker take with a single procedure? How much human energy was expended within each task? Observation of minute details and meticulous measurement provided Taylor with strategies for efficient work habits that greatly advanced productivity.

Observation and measurement are what research psychology is all about, and achievements in applying these skills have brought monumental results. Like Taylor, Swiss psychologist Jean Piaget (1896–1980) systematically observed aspects of everyday life that others overlooked; in Piaget's case, those aspects had to do with children at play and in other interactions and activities. Through years of experiments, interviews, and direct observation, in which he identified distinct stages in the unfolding of young lives, Piaget advanced the discipline of developmental psychology to its current foundational role in childhood education and behavioral psychology.

How might a psychology student go about observing an aspect of life today? You could start by simply looking around. What do you see as you drive to class or ride the subway? What's the climate at Starbucks, the atmosphere in government class, the energy in the student union?

But wait. Maybe there's a better approach than a shot in the dark. Suppose you are new to baseball but find you like it a lot. You already go to the occasional game and enjoy it, but you have never played on any formally organized team. You decide, therefore, that you want to study the interactional dynamics of baseball, the teams, the crowds, the hot dog vendors.

Your first thought is to get some books on baseball and read them, but that's no fun, so you opt to dive right into the game. You could start out by attending a game of collegiate or professional baseball and taking notes. That's fine, but suppose you attend a Chicago Cubs game in the company of a former Cubs player. As you watch the game you see a high home run, and you say, "Wow, I could never get under the ball like that." The player replies, "That's because you would aim for the bottom of the ball. If you want to hit the bottom, aim for the top." As the game progresses, the player points out a dozen other very subtle (and often counterintuitive) techniques employed by professional players. You get him to talk about life with the team, what motivates the players, who has influence, what to watch for in a close match. At your next baseball game you see much more than you did before.

You can learn a lot from an experienced observer.

Consider another example. Movies provide some enlightening examples of veteran professionals mentoring novices. In the 2001 movie *Spy Game*, Robert Redford plays Nathan Muir, a seasoned Central Intelligence Agency spy recruiting a young officer for the Agency. As they sit in a bar in a European city, the spy gives the recruit, Tom Bishop, played by Brad Pitt, an initial lesson in professional observation skills:

MUIR.   Every building, every room, every situation, is a snapshot. While I am sitting here talking to you, I am also checking the room, memorizing the people, what they are wearing. Then I ask the question, "What's wrong with this picture? Anything suspect?" You've got to see it, assess it, and dismiss most of it without looking. Without thinking.

BISHOP.   Without thinking?

MUIR.   It's just like breathing. You breathe, don't you?[1]

---

[1] Wick, D., & Abraham, M. (Producers), & Scott, T. (Director). (2001). *Spy game*. U.S.: Beacon Pictures.

The spy then points out small peculiarities about people in the room that the recruit had not noticed: the man in a dark suit standing passively in the back, the guy holding a menu but not reading it, the woman leaving a table abruptly. The agent asks the recruit if each of them poses a possible threat or serves as a source of information.

It just makes common sense. If you want to supplement your stamp collection, bring your uncle Harry, the philatelist, to the store. If that spot on your right arm troubles you, ask your dermatologist. And if you want some depth of insight about how to professionally observe a person in emotional distress, talk to a counseling psychologist.

Read&Write 5.2   Interview a Counseling Psychologist

If you want to gain some valuable information from an interview, go prepared. Request an appointment time at the interviewee's convenience. Before you go to the interview, generate a list of thoughtfully prepared, open-ended questions. These should help you define beforehand what you really want to know and increase the chances you will get it. You may want to start with a bit of personal information from your interviewee. Here are some possible questions:

- What led you to become a psychologist? Is your profession what you originally expected it to be?
- What interests you about counseling? What types of clients do you find most interesting?
- What are the most important talents and skills for conducting a successful counseling practice?
- What do you try to achieve in your counseling sessions?
- As you observe your clients, what do you look for?
- What have you learned about what body language communicates?
- Do you have techniques for getting clients to divulge things that afflict them?
- How do you know when to press for information and when to draw back?
- What sorts of things can I (the interviewer) do in college to hone my observation skills?

Dress appropriately for the interview. Take lots of notes if you've asked for and received permission to do so. This is important: immediately after the interview, rewrite your notes, adding ideas and insights you have gained. Then write an essay in which you describe the content of your conversation, the insights you gained in the process, your evaluation of the experience, and ideas to improve your skills for your next interview.

6

READ AND WRITE

PROFESSIONALLY

AND CRITICALLY

6.1   READ AND WRITE QUALITATIVE SCHOLARLY ARTICLES IN PSYCHOLOGY

What is *qualitative* scholarship?

In our era of dizzying digital development it may be unwise to assume that arithmetical measurement has its limits. Today your iPhone can take an excellent photo of a prospective date, but it can't tell you how interested he or she is in you. Does your photo subject's enigmatic smile mean you are all right for an off-night, or is it a signal that he or she is playing hard to get? Someday your iPhone will tell you these things and more, because people are now conducting qualitative studies to discover insights about what questions have to be asked to develop new iPhone capabilities.

Consider another example. Today we can easily measure the height, volume, circumference, temperature, density, and aridity of Oregon's Mount Hood. But how do we measure its beauty? Perhaps Google Earth can model what the anticipated environmental effects would be if Mount Hood were to suddenly evaporate. But what unanticipated effects might the mountain's disappearance precipitate? Might there be a crop failure in the Congo or a sudden loss of volume in the Mississippi River? *Qualitative research* is what we do when the knowledge we want is not easy to quantify. Whereas good quantitative research brings us precise answers, good qualitative research helps us discover new interesting questions we have not thought to ask.

Qualitative research techniques are semistructured and more in-depth than quantitative methods. Psychologists who utilize a qualitative approach are not interested in calibrating precisely their subjects' thoughts or actions according to some absolute scale. They structure their research so that subjects can describe thoughts, feelings, and experiences in their own words, or so that the subjects can behave naturally in the social setting being studied. Some of the methods used by qualitative researchers include structured observation, participant observation, interviews, and life histories.

If the research you are conducting is not intended to limit its subjects' behavior or the conditions under which they respond, then the qualitative approach offers a real advantage over quantitative methodology. This is especially true in situations in which social status puts constraints on subjects' freedom to respond. We know that when someone has power over us, we feel less free to respond as we really feel. But when asked the same questions by a social researcher with no ability or desire to configure our responses, we usually feel comfortable telling it as we see it. This is one reason that a well-designed and -administered qualitative study can elicit the in-depth responses that are more likely to give us the full range of meanings we desire in describing a given social setting.

Qualitative research has some disadvantages. The ability to generalize the findings to other populations is limited because (1) the data are not quantified; (2) the samples tend to be nonprobability, that is, not susceptible to statistical analysis; and (3) the conclusions are very specific to the individual or group(s) being studied. If you are interviewing psychologists about causes of stress in their clients' lives and asking them to give in-depth responses to open-ended questions, the findings are limited to the setting that you are assessing. This sort of limitation often occurs with qualitative research. Therefore, qualitative methods are usually applied when we want to better understand some particular aspect of a given clinical or interpersonal setting. We also apply this type of research when our goal is to allow theoretical arguments to emerge and expand.

One of the most common forms of qualitative research in psychology (and many other academic disciplines such as law, business, and medicine) is the *case study*. A case study is an in-depth investigation of a person or a social unit such as a family or group of friends, undertaken to identify the factors that influence the manner in which the person or unit functions. Sigmund Freud conducted several famous case studies, including "Little Hans," a boy who was terrified of horses, and the "Rat Man," a man who had terrifying fantasies about rats. Psychologists have used the case histories of mental patients for many years to support or refute a particular theory. The success of this type of research depends heavily on the open-mindedness, sensitivity, insights, and integrative abilities of the investigator.

Case studies fulfill many educational objectives in the social sciences. As a student in a psychology course, you may write a case study in order to improve your ability to do the following:

- carefully and objectively analyze information
- solve problems effectively
- present your ideas in clear written form to a specific audience

Genograms

Genograms are a type of case study used in many professions for a variety of purposes. For college students they provide an especially convenient opportunity to conduct immediately practical qualitative research.

Psychologists who study family systems have found that the patterns of interactions among the members of our families significantly influence our emotions and the decisions we make in life. Writing a genogram paper will help you gain a better understanding of the interactional patterns of your own family and the ways in which these patterns have influenced you. In addition, if you are studying to become a psychologist, you may find the genogram to be a helpful diagnostic and therapeutic tool.

A genogram is a visual map of a family's relational, emotional, and biographical history. A completed genogram provides a summary of a family's history, which helps people understand complex and often vague patterns of family interaction. You may have always wondered, for example, why Aunt Sally went away for four years and no one ever answered your questions about her absence, or why your cousin Jane always seems to get more attention than you do at family gatherings. A genogram can help answer such questions.

Genograms have two parts. The first is a chart made up of symbols that represent at least three generations of your family members and the types of relationships among them. The second part of a genogram is a written story that explains the relationships among the people who are represented as symbols on the chart.

When you create a genogram you give yourself two views of your family.

The first view is *vertical*, that is, multigenerational. This means that your genogram includes three generations:

- You and your siblings
- Your parents and their siblings
- Your grandparents and their siblings

At any of these levels, you can also add other important people such as a "nanny" or anyone else who was considered part of the family.

The second view is *horizontal*, which means that you see what is going on within one generation, such as among your own brothers and sisters. You will write your genogram as if you were writing a story about your family. Storytelling and written histories have provided the tradition upon which the genogram is developed. Some families have well-developed traditions of storytelling that, at their best, entertain, teach, and guide. Your family story may have heroes and people who provided inspiration for you when you were growing up. At its worst, storytelling that demeans other family members can contribute to shame, misunderstanding, and alienation between members. Even if storytelling is not a conscious tradition in your family, chances are, with a little coaxing, you can remember many stories about your family.

Purpose   A genogram may change your life by increasing your understanding of yourself and your family. Beyond the boundaries of your family, a genogram can help you understand how your neighborhood and the city or town in which it is located have influenced your life. Because a genogram describes interactions among family members, it can illuminate your relationships with your girlfriend or boyfriend as well as your relationships with employers and employees. For example, if you have a parent who was punitive, you are likely to perceive interactions with your teacher, coach, or employer as being potentially hurtful. In contrast, a nurturing relationship with a caregiver can often contribute to the formation of healthy adult relationships.

Read&Write 6.1   Write a Genogram as a Personal Case Study

The purpose of this exercise is to show you how to use and understand the potential of the genogram. It will become an important tool should you go on to become a counselor or a psychologist and grow more adept at using the genogram therapeutically and interpretively. In medicine, a genogram provides a concise picture of the path of disease within a family. In psychotherapy, akin to its use in medicine, a genogram maps the history of adaptive and maladaptive patterns of behavior. Your vision and understanding of these patterns can be broadened and enhanced by the display of multigenerational history that your completed genogram provides.

Researchers have found that certain patterns of behavior and certain ways of thinking seem to be passed along from one generation to the next, often without much conscious awareness. By charting the members of your family back in time, starting with yourself and going back through three generations, and by using the tools and techniques that follow in this chapter, you will find new ways of understanding connections between a current situation, question, or problem and the ways in which that same situation evolved among your family members in other generations or settings. You may find new insights into how you think about problems or discover how much you resemble someone else in your family, such as the paternal grandmother you never knew. A genogram can give you a chance to decide if the past is indeed a prologue to the future.

How to Write a Genogram Paper

There are five basic steps in writing a genogram. Since each segment builds upon the previous one, you should follow the steps as outlined below:

1. List the members of your family.
2. Draw an initial diagram.
3. Write a narrative description of your diagram.
4. Add additional symbols and information to your diagram.
5. Interpret your diagram.

Step 1: List the Members of Your Family   This may seem simple at first glance, but some of you may have grown up in foster homes, with grandparents, in an orphanage, or with aunts or neighbors. The point is that you should include anyone you consider to be a member of your "family."

Two basic principles should guide your thinking about whom to include in your family. First, include those people who are in true blood relationship to you. There may be cases in which these people are not available to you. They may be dead, missing, or otherwise unknown to you, but include them anyway. Second, include those people who raised you, even if those people are not blood relatives. You may have more than one set of parents on your genogram. If you were adopted and know your biological parents as well as your adoptive parents, include them.

The following list attempts to enumerate all the possible people to include in your genogram:

Yourself

Brothers and sisters: Include natural, adopted, foster, step, half, and anyone else in your generation who might have lived with you, such as a cousin, an orphan your family took in, or an abandoned neighbor.

Your parental generation: Include your biological parents, stepparents, foster parents, adoptive parents, and anyone else who acted in a parental role. If you grew up in a group home, for example, you may have related to someone in that setting as a parent (for example, clergy, house parent, or counselor).

Your parents' siblings: Include your aunts and uncles—natural, step, adoptive, foster, and other. Add anyone else whom you called "aunt" or "uncle" but who were not blood relatives.

Your grandparents' generation: Include your grandparents—natural, step, adoptive, foster, and other. Add anyone else you considered a grandparent who was not a blood relative.

Step 2: Draw an Initial Diagram   Draw your initial or first-draft diagram on a sheet of 8.5-by-11-inch paper.

You will eventually add additional information to this diagram in order to produce your final diagram, but your first diagram will include much of the most essential information.

Instead of drawing stick figures or caricatures of your family members, you will use symbols that represent them. The symbols used in genograms have evolved since Murray Bowen originated them in the late 1970s as a part of his pioneering work in family therapy.[1] The symbols used in this text are adapted from those developed by the Task Force of the North American Primary Care Research Group, a group of family therapists and family physicians chaired by M. McGoldrick.[2] The group attempted to create some standardization of symbols for a common language among therapists and physicians. Figure 6.1 provides most of the symbols you will you need to begin construction of the genogram.

Figure 6.2 is a sample diagram that illustrates how these basic symbols might be arranged to represent a hypothetical family we will call the Smiths. The author of the dia-

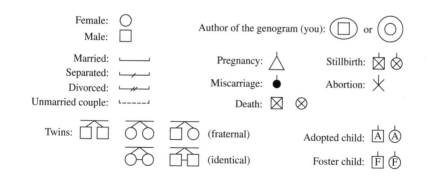

FIGURE 6.1

[1] Bowen, M. (1978). *Family therapy in clinical practice*. Northvale, NJ: Jason Aronson.
[2] McGoldrick, M., & Gerson, R. (1986). *Genograms in family assessment*. New York, NY: Norton.

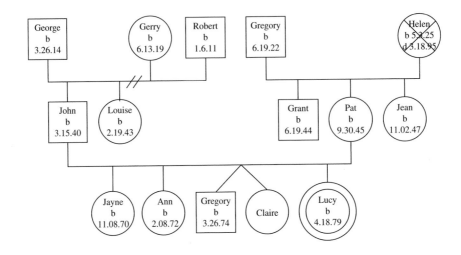

FIGURE 6.2

gram, Lucy Smith, charted her brothers and sisters, parents, paternal grandparents, and maternal grandparents. Notice that the paternal line is usually on the left, the maternal line is usually on the right, and the oldest child is at the far left, with younger siblings on the right.

Now it is your turn. Take a piece of paper and draw your own diagram. Place the paper lengthwise as you work. About two inches from the bottom edge draw a horizontal line where you will put yourself and your siblings (see figure 6.1). Allow about two inches for your parents' generation and another two inches for the grandparents. You may need to play around with the spacing on some scrap paper at first, to get the symbols in reasonable balance with each other. The purpose of making the final chart tidy is to be able to write in figures and names and dates without making the genogram illegible. Spacing will also be a challenge in the cases of multiple stepparents.

After you have drawn the symbols for your family members, label yourself by name and age and do the same for any siblings placed on the same line as yourself. Now move up to your parents' generation, and then to grandparents, giving names and ages (see figure 6.2).

Step 3: Write a Narrative Description of Your Diagram   Your next step is to write a story—a narrative description of your diagram. Tell the story of your life and your family by describing the people represented by the symbols on the diagram. Feel free to add additional symbols and other pertinent information to your diagram (see figure 6.3).

You will probably find that you are missing some important information, such as the date of birth or death of a relative. As you write, compile a list of the pieces of missing information so that you will be able to get this information when you have completed the initial draft of your narrative.

Begin your narrative by introducing yourself and, in a paragraph or so, telling your readers about the most important events in your life. For example, you might begin by saying, "I am 19 years old and the youngest of four children." Then continue by introducing and describing the members of your family. In addition to their names and ages, write such information as their places and dates of birth, their marital status with dates, and any

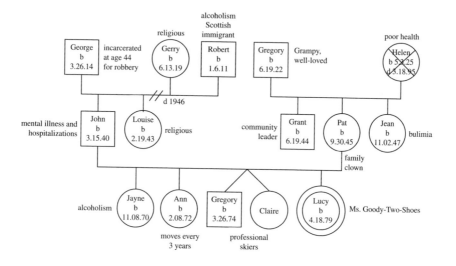

FIGURE 6.3

children they might have (listed in birth order with gender and dates). If deaths in the family were the result of other than natural causes, indicate those causes. Add education levels, occupations, and religious or spiritual affiliations. Fill in as many of these details as you know now, while developing a list of questions to ask later. Suggestions for gathering data are in step 4. Continue your description with information about your siblings before moving on to your parents' and grandparents' generations. The challenge is to make the narrative flow as a story about several very interesting people. When you feel tempted just to list the details, recall the last time you read a boring piece of work, and be creative with your information!

As you write, add depth to your narrative by including details that begin to show the presence of any family patterns. Much in the same way that a jigsaw puzzle begins to make sense when enough of the pieces are in place, so family habits, preferences, or patterns may emerge as you develop your story. Include in your narrative anything that you think is meaningful. Consider including the following types of information to the extent that they are relevant to your family, but do not feel confined to these suggestions:

1. *Family relocation.* Did anyone in your family move to the United States from a foreign country? How often and at what ages did you move while growing up? How did moving affect extended family or other members within the family? For example, did moving bring on a clinical depression for Grandma? Was moving associated with job loss, loss of family members, better pay or living conditions?

2. *Health history.* What effect did ill or robust health have on your family? Include such conditions as alcoholism, eating disorders, and mental or physical illness, and such activities as fitness exercises and amateur or professional sports. How did family members respond to these conditions and activities? For instance, did they refuse to talk about health problems? Did they get outside or professional help? Did they leave the family or provide care?

3. *Incarcerations.* How do family members respond to the prison sentence of a relative? Do they move away from, socially withdraw from, ignore, or visit and support that person? Do they become social activists for prison reform?

4. *Family and community relationships.* How do family members get along day to day in their jobs and communities? Have you heard family stories about Auntie Charisse, who never missed a day of work in her life? Or what about Grandpa, who always played Santa Claus each year at the elementary school and who, until he died at 91, showed up at school each May Day to fly kites with the third-graders? Perhaps your younger sister has trouble keeping a job for more than six months; how do you account for that, and what does your family say? Does anyone else in the family have a similar problem? How do community members see your family members? In other words, are they thought of as hard-working, fickle, upstanding, unreliable?

At this point, your job is to write information about life among the members of your family using the foregoing as a guide. If there are unique qualities about your family, please add them. Try to be alert to coincidences and mindful of any repeating patterns of behavior, attitudes, or values.

As you write, address the questions within one generation; then move on to those within the second and third generations. You will be describing how your family responds to major changes as well as garden-variety joys and disappointments. If a common theme is strong in your family, organize the story around how that theme operates across generations, and provide comparisons of one generation with the others. For example, you may notice that all the women in your family have unusual physical talents, starting with your maternal grandmother, who was a ballet dancer; your mother, who continued her downhill-ski racing career into her late thirties; and your kid sister, who is the Northeastern billiards champion in the under-20-year-old division. The point here is to explore the commonalities and differences within the generations of your family.

Step 4: Add Additional Symbols and Information to Your Diagram   In your paper, you can indicate six qualities of relationship among people represented on the diagram: close, very close, conflict, irritated affection, distance, and cutoff. A *close relationship* exists between people who like each other and are caring and supportive. A *very close relationship* is characterized by such overinvolvement between two family members that neither one has a clear and separate identity. A *conflict* happens when someone is not getting along well with another family member. Most observers can experience the tension between these two family members while in their presence. There is disagreement, discomfort, and dislike. We might add here that the conflict could be between, say, your parent and a former spouse, even though they are no longer in the same household.

An *irritated affection* describes disagreement, agitation, and discomfort between two people, but without the element of disliking each other. This kind of relationship has a contentious quality of bickering and arguing that masks unexpressed affection. In contrast, the quality of *distance* in a family relationship reflects the desire of one member to avoid contact with another out of apathy rather than a need to conceal affection. Finally, a *cutoff* is a term coined to describe an abrupt break with another family member. Unlike an apathetic, distance-type relationship, a cutoff is decisive and often negatively charged insofar as emotions are concerned. A person may have very strong feelings for another yet will deny any resolution of those feelings by running away or claiming no connection. For example, is there anyone in your family who has moved far away and refuses to return? Is there still a charged emotional connection evident whenever this person's name comes up?[3]

---

[3]   McGoldrick, M., & Gerson, R. (1986). *Genograms in family assessment.* New York, NY: Norton; Marlin, E. (1989). *Genograms.* Chicago, IL: Contemporary Books.

Using figure 6.4 as a model, add these symbols to your existing diagram according to your perceptions of familial relationships.

By looking at the strength and nature of relationships, it is easy to see how disconnected or connected the family is. Unlike the objective, factual information of step 1 or the details of step 3, emotional distance is a more subjective assessment. By graphically mapping these qualities of relating, the genogram at this stage (see figure 6.5) facilitates a view of how family patterns replicate themselves across many generations, thereby providing you with the perspective you need to make some interpretations.

We mentioned before that as you write, you may find that you do not have some necessary pieces of information. As a member of your family, you have the most direct access to the information you want. However, that access is not always as easy as it might seem. You might be reluctant to ask for what you want due to things you have learned about your family by growing up in it, like knowing never to ask Dad about the war years or not talking to Mom about her first marriage. These secret areas are often the very ones you are doing a genogram about in the first place, because they represent gaps in your understanding of your family and your place in the family.

This is as good a place as any to alert you to some pitfalls you may encounter while writing a genogram. Asking questions may require care and consideration. For example, a colleague working on a genogram shared the following concern: "Asking questions could be awful! My mother's father was executed in a Russian prison camp. Bringing it up would

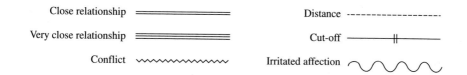

FIGURE 6.4

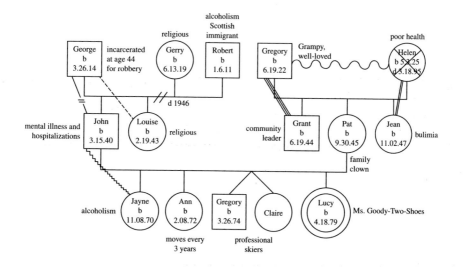

FIGURE 6.5

make her go to pieces." When you know an issue is sensitive, use wisdom to guide your inquiry. However, you may stumble into an issue that catches you by surprise because you knew nothing about it. If you inadvertently create a problem, ask other members of your family to help you. Our colleague may have needed to calm down her mother, remaining with her for a while and asking others to help keep an eye on her. If you are uneasy with a face-to-face meeting with a family member, here are a few alternative ideas: Write down the questions you want answered and mail them to the relative. Have the person tape record the replies and send you the tape. Another idea may be to ask your questions over the phone.

Choose a good time to broach the subject with parents or siblings. Explain that you have a class assignment and need their help. Depending on the climate in your family, you might tell them you are trying to understand some aspects of yourself or of your own behavior. Ask permission to ask them questions and to record their answers. Getting the information you want is sometimes a challenge that requires persistence and creativity on your part. One student researcher, for example, had the idea that his family was quite open to talking, but he ran into uncharacteristic silence from his mother when he asked about bad crop years on the potato farm while his mother was growing up. Another researcher's grandmother was happy to sit with her and talk about her childhood—until the researcher turned on the recorder! At that moment the grandmother required reassurance about the private nature of the recording, and she needed help in getting used to the sound of her recorded voice. Likewise you, too, may face unexpected reticence from a family member or two while collecting information for your genogram.

It is important always to approach your family members with respect and accept a "no, thank you," if that is their wish at the time. Don't be afraid, however, to ask again at some other time. Talking about family business can threaten to expose private fears or trigger a desire to protect someone. If your requests to talk are rejected by some family members, go on to others, perhaps siblings or cousins. At times, and with certain issues, the farther away from the "heart" of the family you go, the easier it is to find members who will talk.

Often, by interviewing various members of the family, you begin to perceive a different picture from the one you have held. Perhaps you can think of an example right now of two relatives who each maintain a totally different view of a third relative. Relationship to that third relative, age differences, and intergenerational effects add to the challenge of sorting out the new information you get and the challenge of writing the information down clearly.

Friends are a good source to bring balance to the myopic view you can develop of your own family. Friends can help temper outrageous family reactions, and friends can also point out rough places to which some family members are blind. Family Bibles or other documents are great sources of information about details such as names, dates, marriages, births, and deaths, though they provide little in the way of information about the quality of a relationship or its strength. Newspaper articles about your family or a member of the family can be insightful. Personal diaries (read with permission!), essays, stories, and even artwork can be a window to thoughts.

Step 5: Interpret Your Diagram The purpose of this step is for you to make sense for yourself of what you have learned about your family and write it down. The task is interpretive and, as it is your own perception of how things are, your brothers or sisters may not agree with what you write. As you interpret your diagram, consider the following questions.

What kinds of relationships exist between you and any of your siblings? Between you and either (or any) of your parents? Between you and grandparents? What relationships do you observe among other family members?

Are there any "triangles"? Just suppose that your younger brother is very close to your mother and in conflict with your father. Connect the relationship between mother and father to create a *graphic triangle*. What do you observe about that relationship, and what effect does it have on you or another family member?

Have you discovered any family myths? Who knows about the myths and who does not? Are there tendencies for certain people to be rescuers, fighters, peacemakers? Are the myths retold at family gatherings, at cocktail parties, on the golf course, at pubs, with men only or women only? Are there any themes to the family myths?

Have you discovered any secrets? Who else knows, and who does not know? Here's an example: A client once shared with her therapist her amazement at finding out as a young adult that her mother was an alcoholic. For years the client had thought her mother was "in a funny mood" or "crazy." The secret was so secure that the family did not inform her earlier. Does information travel a predictable path through your family? In other words, does your mother first tell news, say, to your older sister, who tells her middle son, who then tells you?

Is birth order important in your family? Are firstborn children in each generation treated similarly? Do they act similarly? Are terms such as "Son" or "Junior" or "Baby" used with certain children? Is a pattern revealed in which a particular birth-order child seems to receive special attention, whether positive or negative? Is anyone left out of the loop? Are there several husbands or wives with the same first name? Or with the same jobs?

Are there any cutoff roots? What are your observations of family members who don't speak to each other? Have family members moved away and not been seen again? What words are used by the family to describe these relatives or the situations surrounding their move away from the family?

The final paragraph of your paper should summarize the insights you have gained and the conclusions that you have drawn about the relationships in your family and how they affect you.

The Components of a Genogram Paper

A genogram paper has these components:

- Title page
- Body of the paper, which includes:

  - A narrative that describes the people and relationships indicated on your genogram
  - A narrative that interprets the relationships indicated in the genogram

- Appendix, consisting of your final family diagram (genogram), to which you refer while writing your paper.

6.2 CRITIQUE AN ACADEMIC ARTICLE

An *article critique* is a paper that evaluates an article published in an academic journal. A good critique tells the reader what point the article is trying to make and how convincingly it makes this point. Writing an article critique achieves three purposes. First, it provides you with an understanding of the information contained in a scholarly article. Second, it provides you with an opportunity to apply and develop your critical thinking skills as you attempt to evaluate a psychologist's work. Third, it helps you improve your own writing skills as you attempt to describe the selected article's strengths and weaknesses so that your readers can clearly understand them.

Preparing to Write an Article Critique

The first step in writing an article critique is to select an appropriate article. Unless your instructor specifies otherwise, select an article from a scholarly journal, such as the *American Psychologist*, the *Journal of Counseling Psychology*, or the *Journal of Consulting and Clinical Psychology*, and not a popular or journalistic publication, such as *Time* or *Psychology Today*. Your instructor may also accept appropriate articles from academic journals in other disciplines.

The second step is to browse titles in the journal until you find a topic that interests you. Writing a critique will be much more satisfying if you have an interest in the topic. Hundreds of interesting journal articles are published every year. The following articles, for example, appeared in a single issue (May–June 2016) of the journal *American Psychologist* (volume 71, number 4), a special issue titled *Aging in America: Perspectives from Psychological Science*:[4]

"Psychology's Contribution to the Well-Being of Older Americans" (Margaret Gatz, Michael A. Smyer, and Deborah A. DiGilio)

"Healthy Cognitive Aging and Dementia Prevention" (Glenn E. Smith)

"Promoting Healthy Aging by Confronting Ageism" (Todd D. Nelson)

"Caregiving Families within the Long-Term Services and Support System for Older Adults" (Sara Honn Qualls)

"Long-Term Care Services and Support Systems for Older Adults: The Role of Technology" (Sara J. Czaja)

"The Complexities of Elder Abuse" (Karen A. Roberto)

"Financial Exploitation, Financial Capacity, and Alzheimer's Disease" (Peter A. Lictenberg)

"The New World of Retirement Income Security In America" (Joseph F. Quinn and Kevin E. Cahill)

"Retirement Security: It's Not Just About the Money" (Jacquelyn Boone James, Christina Matz-Costa, and Michael A. Smyer)

Besides picking an article of interest to you, another consideration in selecting an article is your current level of knowledge. Many psychology students are not knowledgeable about, for example, sophisticated statistical techniques. You may be better prepared to evaluate a sophisticated statistical procedure if you have studied statistics.

Finally, it may be helpful to pick an article that has been written within the last 12 months, because most material in psychology is quickly superseded by new studies. Selecting a recent article will help ensure that you will be engaged in an up-to-date discussion of your topic.

---

[4]   Aging in America: Perspectives from psychological science. (2016, May–June). *American Psychologist.* Retrieved from http://www.apa.org/pubs/journals/special/4017105.aspx

Read&Write 6.2 Critique a Scholarly Psychology Article

The Components of an Article Critique

Now that you have selected your article, the third step is to read your article carefully and begin to write your critique. Following the sections of the article, this critique will consist of five parts:

1. Thesis
2. Methods
3. Evidence of Thesis Support
4. Contribution to the Literature
5. Recommendation

Thesis   The first task is to state the thesis of the article clearly and succinctly. See section 1.1 of this manual, and then locate and state the thesis of the article you are reviewing.

Methods   What methods did the authors use to investigate the topic? In other words, how did the authors go about supporting their thesis? In your critique, carefully answer the following questions:

- Were appropriate methods used? (Did the authors' approach to supporting their thesis make sense?)
- Did the authors employ their selected methods correctly? (Did you discover any errors in the way they conducted their research?)

No matter how professionally a published article is structured and written, there is usually an element or two that could have used some improvement. For example, in the study by B. S. Richie et al., titled "Persistence, Connection, and Passion: A Qualitative Study of the Career Development of Highly Achieving African American–Black and White Women," published in volume 44 of the *Journal of Counseling Psychology*, 125 nationally prominent, highly successful African American women were questioned via a survey format.[5] For the final study, a matched sample of African American women was included to explore the effects of both racism and sexism on career development.

One of the methodological problems with this study is that it was based on one in-depth interview with each woman. Additional sources such as information from diaries, archival documents, or observations might have strengthened the study. Moreover, the sample consisted only of women in the Northeast who were similar in age and developmental phase of life. It may be important, therefore, to test this model with samples representative of other populations.

Evidence of Thesis Support   In your critique, answer the following questions:

- What evidence did the authors present in support of the thesis?
- What are the strengths of the evidence presented?

---

[5] Richie, B. S., et al. (1997, April). Persistence, connection, and passion: A qualitative study of the career development of highly achieving African American–Black and White women. *Journal of Counseling Psychology, 44*(2), 133–148. doi:10.1037/0022-0167.44.2.133

- What are the weaknesses of the evidence presented?
- On balance, how well did the authors support their thesis?

Focusing on finding answers to these questions can help you determine the organization not only of the paper but also of the research on which the paper was based.

Contribution to the Literature   This step will probably require you to undertake some research. Using your library's online catalog, identify articles and books published within the last five years on the subject of your selected article. Browse the titles and read perhaps a half dozen of the publications that appear to provide the best discussion of the topic. In your critique, list the most important of these articles or books that have been published on your topic, and then, with these publications in mind, evaluate the contribution that your selected article makes to a better understanding of its topic.

Recommendation   In this section, clearly summarize your evaluation of the article, answering the following questions for your reader:

Who will benefit from reading this article?

What will the benefit be?

How important and extensive is that benefit?

6.3   WRITE A BOOK REVIEW

Successful book reviews answer three questions:

1. What is the writer of the book trying to communicate?
2. How clearly and convincingly does he or she get this message across to the reader?
3. Is the message worth reading?

Capable book reviewers of several centuries have answered these three questions well. People who read a book review want to know if a particular book is worth reading, for their own particular purposes, before buying or reading it. These potential readers want to know the book's subject and its strengths and weaknesses, and they want to gain this information as easily and quickly as possible. Your goal in writing a book review, therefore, is to help people efficiently decide whether to buy or read a book. Your immediate objectives may be to please your instructor and get a good grade, but you are most likely to meet these objectives if you focus on a book review's audience: people who want help in selecting books to buy or read. In the process of writing a book review that reaches this primary goal, you will also

- Learn about the book you are reviewing
- Learn about professional standards for book reviews in psychology
- Learn the essential steps of book reviewing that apply to any academic discipline

This final objective, learning to review a book properly, has more applications than you may at first imagine. First, it helps you focus quickly on the essential elements of a book and draw from a book its informational value for yourself and others. Some of the most successful people in government, business, and the professions speed-read several books a week, more for the knowledge they contain than for enjoyment. These readers then apply this knowledge to substantial advantage in their professions. It is normally not wise to speed-read a book you are reviewing because you are unlikely to gain enough information to evaluate it fairly from such a fast reading. Writing book reviews, however, helps you become proficient in quickly sorting out valuable information from material that is not. The ability to make such discriminations is a fundamental ingredient in management and professional success.

In addition, writing book reviews for publication allows you to participate in the discussions of the broader intellectual and professional community of which you are a part. People in law, medicine, teaching, engineering, administration, and other fields are frequently asked to write book reviews to help others assess newly released publications.

Elements of a Book Review

Your first sentence should entice people to read your review. A crisp summary of what the book is about entices your readers because it lets them know that you can quickly and clearly come to the point. They know that their time and effort will not be wasted in an attempt to wade through vague prose in hopes of finding out something about the book. Your opening statement can be engaging and catchy, but be sure that it provides an accurate portrayal of the book in one crisp statement.

Your review should allow the reader to join you in examining the book. Tell the reader what the book is about. Let the reader know in your first paragraph exactly what you think the book accomplishes.

But be careful. Write about what is actually in the book, not what you think is probably there or ought to be there. Do not explain how you would have written the book, but instead how the author wrote it. Describe the book in clear, objective terms. Tell enough about the content to identify the author's major points.

Clarify the book's value and contribution to the field of psychological study by defining (1) what the author is attempting to do and (2) how the author's work fits within current similar efforts in the discipline of psychology or scholarly inquiry in general. Place the work within the context of current similar writing in the field. This step will very probably send you to the library or the library's online catalog, where you'll make a survey of other publications on the subject of the book you are reviewing, looking for congruencies and differences of opinion. It is likely that the author of the book you are reviewing will help you by naming other works in the field with which he or she agrees or takes issue.

The explication portion of a book review often provides additional information about the author. It would be helpful to know, for example, if the author has written other books on the subject, has developed a reputation for exceptional expertise on a certain issue, or is known to have a particular ideological bias. How would your understanding of this book be changed, for example, if you knew that its author had been a leader of a white supremacist organization? Include information in your book review about the author that helps the reader understand how this book fits within the broader concerns of psychology.

Once you explain what the book is attempting to do, you should tell the reader the extent to which this goal has been met. To evaluate a book effectively, you will need to establish evaluation criteria and then compare the book's content to those criteria. You do not need to define your criteria specifically in your review, but they should be evident to the reader. Your criteria will vary according to the book you are reviewing, and you may discuss them in any order that is helpful to the reader. Consider, however, including the following among the criteria that you establish for your book review:

- How important is the subject to the field of study that is the book's focus?
- How complete and thorough is the author's coverage of the subject?
- How carefully is the author's analysis conducted?
- What are the strengths and limitations of the author's methodology?
- What is the quality of the writing? Is it clear, precise, and interesting?
- How does this book compare with others on the subject?
- What contribution does this book make to its discipline (its field of study)?
- Who will enjoy or benefit from this book?

When giving your evaluations according to these criteria, be specific. If you write, "This is a good book; I liked it very much," you say nothing of interest or value to the reader. Define clearly the content, achievements, and limitations of the book.

Read&Write 6.3   Review a New Psychology Book

Format and Content   Several of the APA's journals (http://www.apa.org) publish book reviews. Peruse several of these through your college library's online catalog, getting a feel for both the format and the content of an effective book review. Then check out http://www.newbooksnetwork.com and select PSYCHOLOGY under the SCIENCE AND TECH tab. You will find brief descriptions of dozens of new books on psychology. Find a book that interests you—one that you can check out from your library. Check out the copy and read and review the book, following the guidelines above.

6.4   WRITE A LITERATURE REVIEW

Your goal in writing a research paper is to provide your readers an opportunity to increase their understanding of the subject you are addressing. They will want the most current and precise information available. Whether you are writing a traditional library research paper or conducting an experiment, you must know what has already been learned in order to give your readers comprehensive and up-to-date information or to add something new to what is already known about the subject. If your topic is the attributes of depression, for example, you will want to find out precisely what attributes have already been identified by people who have done depression research. When you seek this information, you will be conducting a *literature review*, a thoughtful collection and analysis of available information on the topic you have selected for study. It tells you, before you begin your experiments or analyses, what is already known about the subject.

Why do you need to conduct a literature review? It would be embarrassing to spend a lot of time and effort preparing a study only to find that the information you are seeking has already been discovered by someone else. Also, a properly conducted literature review will tell you many things about a particular subject. It will tell you the extent of current knowledge, sources of data for your research, examples of what is *not* known about the subject (which in turn generates ideas for formulating hypotheses), methods that have been used for research, and clear definitions of concepts relevant to your own research.

Sample psychology literature reviews are not difficult to find. A search conducted for this manual through a typical online college-library catalog, with the terms "literature review" and "psychology" entered in the catalog's search engine, revealed a score of recent reviews, including "A Systematic Review of the Literature on Posttraumatic Stress Disorder in Victims of Terrorist Attacks," by María Paz García-Vera, Jesus Sanz, and Sara Gutiérrez, of Universidad Complutense de Madrid, Spain.[6] It is possible to download the entire article in a PDF file. Its abstract begins with the following two sentences: "This article was aimed at systematically reviewing the literature on posttraumatic stress disorder (PTSD) among victims of terrorist attacks. Electronic and hand searches of the literature identified 35 studies addressing PTSD prevalence based on validated diagnostic interviews."

What are the steps for conducting a literature review of a subject in the field of psychology? Suppose that you have decided to research this question: "How will depressed adolescents express their depression in their relationships with their friends?" First, you will need to establish a clear definition of "depression," and then you will need to find a way to identify the ways in which depressed adolescents relate with their friends. Using techniques explained in this and other chapters of this manual, you will begin your research by looking in your college library's online catalog for studies that address your research question or similar questions. You will discover that many studies have been conducted on adolescents and depression.

As you read these studies, you will begin to formulate certain conclusions about the research on your chosen subject. You may well find, for example, that some research methods appear to have produced better results than others. Some studies will be quoted in others many times, some confirming and others refuting what previous studies have done. As you examine these studies you will constantly be making choices, reading very carefully those studies that are highly relevant to your purposes and skimming those of only marginal interest. As you read, constantly ask yourself the following questions:

- How much is known about this subject?
- What is the best available information, and why is it better than other information?
- What research methods have been used successfully in relevant studies?
- What are possible sources of data for further investigation of this topic?
- What important information is still not known, in spite of all previous research?

[6] García-Vera, M. P., Sanz, J., & Gutiérrez, S. (2016, July). A systematic review of the literature on posttraumatic stress disorder in victims of terrorist attacks. *Psychological Reports, 119*(1), 328–359. doi:10.1177/0033294116658243

- Of the methods that have been used for research, which are the most effective for making new discoveries? Are new methods needed?
- How can the concepts being researched be more precisely defined?

You will find that this process, like the research process as a whole, is recursive: insights related to one of the above questions will spark new investigations into others, and these investigations will then bring up a new set of questions, and so on.

Your instructor may request that you include a literature review as a section of the paper that you are writing. Your written literature review may be from one to several pages in length, but it should always answer these questions:

- What specific previously compiled or published studies, articles, or other documents provide the best available information on the selected topic?
- What do these studies conclude about the topic?
- What are the apparent methodological strengths and weaknesses of these studies?
- What remains to be discovered about the topic?
- What appear to be, according to these studies, the most effective methods for developing new information on the topic?

The success of your own research project depends in large part on the extent to which you have carefully and thoughtfully answered these questions.

Read&Write 6.4 Write a Psychology Literature Review

Your task now is to select a topic in psychology and conduct a literature review that includes at least 12 significant published sources.

7

RESEARCH EFFECTIVELY

Preliminary Scholarship

7.1 INSTITUTE AN EFFECTIVE RESEARCH PROCESS

The research paper is where all your skills as an interpreter of details, an organizer of facts and theories, and a writer of clear prose come together. Building logical arguments on the twin bases of fact and hypothesis is the way things are done in psychology, and the most successful psychology students are those who master the art of research.

Students new to the writing of research papers sometimes find themselves intimidated by the job ahead of them. After all, the research paper adds what seems to be an extra set of complexities to the writing process. As any other expository or persuasive paper does, a research paper must present an original thesis using a carefully organized and logical argument. But it also investigates a topic that is outside the writer's own experience. This means that writers must locate and evaluate information that is new, thus, in effect, educating themselves as they explore their topics. A beginning researcher sometimes feels overwhelmed by the basic requirements of the assignment or by the authority of the source material being investigated.

As you begin a research project, it may be difficult to establish a sense of control over the different tasks you are undertaking. You may have little notion of where to search for a thesis or even how to locate the most helpful information. If you do not carefully monitor your own work habits, you may find yourself unwittingly abdicating responsibility for the paper's argument by borrowing it wholesale from one or more of your sources.

Who is in control of your paper? The answer must be you—not the instructor who assigned you the paper, and certainly not the published writers and interviewees whose opinions you solicit. If all your paper does is paste together the opinions of others, it has little use. It is up to you to synthesize an original idea from a judicious evaluation of your source material. At the beginning of your research project, you will, of course, be unsure about many elements of your paper. For example, you will probably not yet have a definitive thesis sentence or even much understanding of the shape of your argument. But you can establish a measure of control over the process you will go through to complete the paper. And if you work regularly and systematically, keeping yourself open to new ideas as they present themselves, your sense of control will grow. Following are some suggestions to help you establish and maintain control of your paper.

Understand Your Assignment

It is possible for a research assignment to go badly simply because the writer did not read the assignment carefully. Considering how much time and effort you are about to put into your project, it is a very good idea to make sure you have a clear understanding of what your instructor wants you to do. Be sure to ask your instructor about any aspect of the assignment that is unclear to you—but only after you have read it carefully. Recopying the assignment in your own handwriting is a good way to start, even though your instructor may have already given it to you in writing. Before you dive into the project, make sure that you have considered the questions listed below.

1. **What is your topic?** The assignment may give you a great deal of specific information about your topic, or you may be allowed considerable freedom in establishing one for yourself. For a behavioral psychology course, your professor may give you a very specific assignment—a paper, for example, examining the effects of natural disasters on the emotional development of children under 12 years of age—or he or she may allow you to choose for yourself the issue that your paper will address. You need to understand the terms, as set up in the assignment, by which you will design your project.

2. **What is your purpose?** Whatever the degree of latitude you are given in the matter of your topic, pay close attention to the way your instructor has phrased the assignment. Is your primary job to *describe* a current situation or to *explain* it? Are you to *compare* treatment options, and if so, to what end?

3. **Who is your audience?** Your own orientation to the paper is profoundly affected by your conception of the audience for whom you are writing. Granted that your main reader is your instructor, who else would be interested in your paper? Are you writing for the readers of a scholarly journal or for the general public? A paper that describes research procedures may justifiably contain much more technical jargon for an audience of psychologists than for students in an introductory psychology course.

4. **What kind of research are you doing?** You will be doing one if not both of the following kinds of research:
   - *Primary research*, which requires you to discover information firsthand, often by conducting experiments or controlled observations. In primary research, you are collecting and sifting through raw data—data that have not already been interpreted by researchers—which you will then study, select, arrange, and speculate on. These raw data may be the text of unaltered observations or numbers derived from experiments. It is important to carefully set up the methods by which you collect your data. Your aim

is to gather the most accurate information possible, from which you or other writers using the material you have uncovered will later make sound observations.

- *Secondary research*, which uses published accounts of primary materials. Although the primary researcher might conduct an experiment in which participants are asked to categorize facial expressions, for example, the secondary researcher will use the material from an already-performed experiment to support a particular thesis. Secondary research, in other words, focuses on interpretations of raw data. Most of your college papers will be based on your use of secondary sources.

Primary Source	Secondary Source
Category totals for responses to facial expressions	A journal article arguing that women interpret certain facial expressions more negatively than men due to cultural biases
A transcript of an interview with a psychologist	A personality assessment of the psychologist based on the interview
Data indicating the number of times a child looked to an adult for reassurance	A paper basing its thesis on the results of the data

Keep Your Perspective

Whichever type of research you perform, you must keep your results in perspective. There is no way that you, as a primary researcher, can be completely objective in your findings. It is not possible to design a questionnaire that will net you absolute truth, nor can you be sure that the opinions you gather in interviews reflect the accurate and unchanging opinions of the people you question. Likewise, if you are conducting secondary research, you must remember that the articles and journals you are reading are shaped by the aims of their writers, who are interpreting primary materials for their own ends. The farther you are removed from a primary source, the greater the possibility for distortion. Your job as a researcher is to be as accurate as possible, which means keeping in view the limitations of your methods and their ends.

In any research project, there will be moments of confusion, but you can prevent this confusion from overwhelming you by establishing an effective research procedure. You need to design a schedule that is as systematic as possible, yet flexible enough so that you do not feel trapped by it. By always showing you what to do next, a schedule will help prevent you from running into dead ends. At the same time, the schedule can help you retain the focus necessary to spot new ideas and new strategies as you work.

Give Yourself Plenty of Time

You may feel like delaying your research for many reasons: unfamiliarity with the library, the press of other tasks, a deadline that seems comfortably far away. But do not allow such factors to deter you. Research takes time. Working in a library seems to speed up the clock, so that the single hour you expected it would take you to find a certain source becomes two. You must allow yourself the time needed not only to find material but also to read it, assimilate it, and set it in the context of your own thoughts. If you delay starting, you may well find yourself distracted by the deadline and having to keep an eye on the clock while trying to make sense of a writer's complicated argument. To stay on track you will need to construct a schedule that contains a list of the components of the project and the dates by which they must be completed.

Read & Write 7.1   Write a Research Proposal

Do you aspire to a professional career? Psychologist? Entrepreneur? Doctor? Lawyer? Engineer? School Principal? Professor? Nurse? Architect? Marketing Director? Executive Director, Nonprofit Organization? Research Director? The ability to write a high-quality *research proposal* may well be one of the most useful and profitable skills you acquire on route to your BA or BS. Research proposals are written by the hundreds in public and private agencies and by innovators and entrepreneurs every day. A long-standing motto of entrepreneurs of all sorts is a simple guide to commercial success: "Find a need and fill it." From the lightbulb to the iPhone, this principle has been a guiding motivation for thousands of successful therapists, inventors, entrepreneurs, CEOs, volunteers, and others. Remember that a *need* is both a problem that someone wants to solve and an opportunity for you to make a contribution by solving it.

How does writing a research proposal foster success in this process? Simple. Most new ventures require *funding*. Most sources of funding (a college research office, government agencies, nonprofit organizations, investors) require you to submit a *plan* or *feasibility study* that demonstrates (1) the need for a particular project, (2) the economic viability of the project, (3) the inclusion of the talent, expertise, and experience needed to successfully undertake the project.

The research proposal is the first step in acquiring funding and/or authorization to conduct the research necessary to affirm the need for and feasibility of the project.

Research proposals, therefore, are sales jobs. Their purpose is to "sell" the belief that a research study needs to be done. Before conducting a research study for a government agency, you will need to convince someone in authority that a study is necessary by accomplishing the following seven tasks:

1. Prove (submit evidence) that the study is necessary.
2. Describe the objectives of the study.
3. Explain how the study will be done.
4. Describe the resources (time, people, equipment, facilities, etc.) that will be needed to do the job.
5. Construct a schedule that states when the project will begin and end, and gives important dates in between.
6. Prepare a project budget that specifies the financial costs and the amount to be billed (if any) to the funding agency.
7. Carefully define what the research project will produce, what kind of study will be conducted, how long it will be, and what it will contain.

The Content of Research Proposals: An Overview   In form, research proposals contain the following four parts:

1. Title page
2. Outline page
3. Text
4. Reference page

An outline of the content of research proposals appears below:

I. Need for a study
   A. An initial description of the current problem
      1. A definition of the problem
      2. A brief history of the problem
      3. The legal framework and institutional setting of the problem
      4. The character of the problem, including its size, extent, and importance
   B. Imperatives
      1. The probable costs of taking no action
      2. The expected benefits of the study
II. Methodology of the proposed study
   A. Project management methods to be used
   B. Research methods to be used
   C. Data analysis methods to be used
III. Resources necessary to conduct the study
   A. Material resources
   B. Human resources
   C. Financial resources
IV. Schedule for the study
V. Budget for the study
VI. Product of the study

A Note on Research Process and Methods   Your research proposal will briefly describe the steps you will take to find, evaluate, and draw conclusions from the information that is pertinent to your study. The research process normally proceeds in these steps:

1. Data (information) collection: gathering the appropriate information
2. Data analysis: organizing the data and determining their meaning or implications
3. Data evaluation: determining what conclusions may be drawn from the data
4. Recommendation: A concise description of the study that needs to be undertaken

A Note on the Anticipated Product of the Study   In the final section of the proposal, you will describe the projected outcomes of your study. In other words, you will tell the persons for whom you are writing the proposal exactly what they will receive when the project is done. If you are writing this paper for a class in clinical psychology, you will probably write something like the following:

The final product will be a research study from 25 to 30 pages in length and will provide an analysis of the problem and an evaluation of alternative new policies that may solve the problem.

7.2 EVALUATE THE QUALITY OF ONLINE AND PRINTED INFORMATION

The saying "Winning isn't everything; it's the only thing" may not have originated with Green Bay Packers coach Vince Lombardi, but he certainly popularized it. In terms of academic scholarship, to say "Credibility isn't everything; it's the only thing" is not an exaggeration, because the importance of what is written cannot be underestimated. All the same, as you write psychology scholarship, assume correctly that if your work lacks credibility, it has no value at all. With this in mind, understand that the credibility of your writing will depend, more than anything else, on the credibility of your sources. Here, therefore, are some guidelines to assess the credibility of the sources you employ in your paper.

The principles to be applied in reading sources of information are much the same whether you read a news article, a blog post, a tweet, or a scholarly article. Here are some general guidelines.

Reputation

In general, reputation of information conforms to a clear hierarchy, described here in descending order of credibility. Here is a list of high-quality sources:

- *Articles in academic journals*, though not foolproof, have a huge credibility advantage. They conform to the research and writing standards explained throughout this manual. They often require months, if not years, to write, allowing for revision and refinement. They often employ a team of several authors, each of whom can assess the quality and accuracy of the others' work. Once submitted to a journal for publication they are distributed (blind) to experts in the articles' topics for review and comment. Once published they are exposed to widespread readership, providing an additional quality filter.

- *Research studies by recognized think tanks* (research institutes) are often of exceptionally high quality. They are not exposed to the same extent of external review prior to publication as academic journals, and the institutions that produce them often have a known ideological perspective. Yet whether they are conservative, liberal, or libertarian in orientation, their writers know that the credibility of their work depends on maintaining consistent high quality.

- *Research studies by government agencies* are much like think tank papers but are likely to be controversial because their findings will always annoy people who are unhappy with their conclusions. They can be very powerful, however, if they are used by presidents or by Congress to adopt particular public policies.

- *Reports in high-quality nonpartisan magazines and television journalism* are often highly reliable in both research and reporting. Examples of sources include periodicals like the *Economist*, the *Atlantic Monthly*, the *New Yorker*, the *American Scholar*, *Foreign Affairs*, *Foreign Policy*, and PBS journalism in features such as *Frontline* and *The American Experience*.

- *Articles in high-quality newspapers*, like the *New York Times*, the *Wall Street Journal*, the *Washington Post*, and the *Christian Science Monitor* cite authoritative sources.

- *Pieces in high-quality partisan magazines* like the *Nation* and the *National Review* can provide relatively reliable, if slanted and selective, information.

Low-quality sources are of several sorts, and all are to be read for quickly secured unverified "facts" and amusement rather than education. Here are some low-quality sources:

- *Wikipedia* provides much information quickly and some tolerable overviews of topics, but it is notoriously vulnerable to people who provide unverified and even false information.
- Partisan blogs, like the *Huffington Post*, are fun and provide an interesting array of perspectives and insights, but any information you find on them must be verified by more credible sources.
- Commercial TV news sources, like CNN, CNBC, and, especially, Fox News are so sensational and clearly biased that their value is little more than entertainment.

The following elements of information sources are essential to assessing content quality:

- *Author.* What are the credentials and reputation of the author of the publication?
- *Information sources.* What sources of information does the author of a particular article use? Are these sources recognized individuals or institutions?
- *Writing quality.* Is the article well written? Is it clear and cogent? Does it use a lot of jargon? Can you understand it?
- *Quantity of information.* Is the article sufficiently comprehensive to substantiate its thesis?
- *Unsupported assumptions.* Beware statements like this: "Statistics prove that hospitals in urban areas provide better care than rural facilities." What statistics? Does the article identify them?
- *Balance.* Does the article cover all relevant aspects of a subject?

Develop a Working Bibliography

As you begin your research, you will look for published sources—essays, books, or interviews with experts—that may help you. This list of potentially useful sources is your *working bibliography*. There are many ways to develop this bibliography. The cataloging system in your library will give you sources, as will the published bibliographies in your field. The general references in which you did your background reading may also list such works, and each specialized book or essay you find will have a bibliography that its writer used, which may be helpful to you.

It is from your working bibliography that you will select the items for the bibliography that will appear in the final draft of your paper. Early in your research, you will not know which of the sources will help you and which will not, but it is important to keep an accurate description of each entry in your working bibliography so that you will be able to tell clearly which items you have investigated and which you will need to consult again. As you make your list of potential sources, be sure to include, about each one, all the bibliographical information that you would need to relocate the source, should you have to do so later on in the production of your paper. It's a very good idea to arrange this information according to the bibliographical format you are required to follow in your final draft, using the proper punctuation. (Chapter 3 describes in detail the bibliographical formats most often required for psychology papers.)

Request Needed Information

In the course of your research, you may need to consult a source that is not immediately available to you. You might find that a packet of potentially useful information may be obtained from a government agency or public interest group in Washington, DC. Or you may discover that a needed book is not owned by your university library or by any other local library. In such situations, it may be tempting to disregard the hard-to-acquire source because of the difficulty of consulting it. If you ignore this material, however, you are not doing your job.

It is vital that you take steps to acquire the needed data. In the first case mentioned above, you can simply write to the Washington, DC, agency or interest group; in the second, you may use your library's interlibrary loan procedure to obtain the book. Remember all the technology aids you have at your command—including email, phone, and Internet—to help you secure potentially helpful source material. Remember, too, that many businesses and government agencies want to share their information with interested citizens; some have employees or entire departments whose job is to facilitate communication with the public. Be as specific as possible when asking for such information. It is a good idea, in your request for help, to outline your own project briefly—in no more than a few sentences—to allow the respondent to determine the types of information that will be useful to you.

Never let the immediate unavailability of a source stop you from trying to consult it. And be sure to begin the job of locating and acquiring such long-distance material as soon as possible, to allow for the various delays that often occur.

Read&Write 7.2 Locate and List a Dozen High-Quality Sources

Assume you are going to write a 10-page paper on a topic of your choice. Locate and list, in APA bibliographical format, a dozen high-quality sources for your paper.

8

BRAIN AND BODY

8.1 BIOLOGICAL PSYCHOLOGY

In 2016 the U.S. Global Change Research Program (http://www.globalchange .gov) issued a comprehensive report on global climate change titled *The Impacts of Climate Change on Human Health in the United States: A Scientific Assessment.*[1] This report contains nine chapters, as follows:

1. Climate Change and Human Health
2. Temperature-Related Death and Illness
3. Air Quality Impacts
4. Extreme Events
5. Vector-Borne Diseases
6. Water-Related Illness
7. Food Safety, Nutrition, and Distribution
8. Mental Health and Well-Being
9. Populations of Concern

Chapter 8, "Mental Health and Well-Being," presents four key findings:

- Exposure to Disasters Results in Mental Health Consequences
    Key Finding 1: Many people exposed to climate-related or weather-related disasters experience stress and serious mental health consequences. Depending on the type of the disaster, these consequences include posttraumatic stress disorder (PTSD), depression, and general anxiety, which often occur at the same time [Very High Confidence]. The majority of affected people recover over time, although a

---

[1] USGCRP. (2016). *The impacts of climate change on human health in the United States: A scientific assessment.* Washington, DC: U.S. Global Change Research Program. Retrieved from http://dx.doi .org/10.7930/J0R49NQX

significant proportion of exposed individuals develop chronic psychological dysfunction [High Confidence].

- Specific Groups of People Are at Higher Risk

  Key Finding 2: Specific groups of people are at higher risk for distress and other adverse mental health consequences from exposure to climate-related or weather-related disasters. These groups include children, the elderly, women (especially pregnant and post-partum women), people with preexisting mental illness, the economically disadvantaged, the homeless, and first responders [High Confidence]. Communities that rely on the natural environment for sustenance and livelihood, as well as populations living in areas most susceptible to specific climate change events, are at increased risk for adverse mental health outcomes [High Confidence].

- Climate Change Threats Result in Mental Health Consequences and Social Impacts

  Key Finding 3: Many people will experience adverse mental health outcomes and social impacts from the threat of climate change, the perceived direct experience of climate change, and changes to one's local environment [High Confidence]. Media and popular culture representations of climate change influence stress responses and mental health and well-being [Medium Confidence].

- Extreme Heat Increases Risks for People with Mental Illness

  Key Finding 4: People with mental illness are at higher risk for poor physical and mental health due to extreme heat [High Confidence]. Increases in extreme heat will increase the risk of disease and death for people with mental illness, including elderly populations and those taking prescription medications that impair the body's ability to regulate temperature [High Confidence].[2]

Chapter 9, "Populations of Concern," presents the following key findings:

- Vulnerability Varies Over Time and Is Place-Specific

  Key Finding 1: Across the United States, people and communities differ in their exposures, their inherent sensitivity, and their adaptive capacity to respond to and cope with climate change related health threats [Very High Confidence]. Vulnerability to climate change varies across time and location, across communities, and among individuals within communities [Very High Confidence].

- Health Impacts Vary with Age and Life Stage

  Key Finding 2: People experience different inherent sensitivities to the impacts of climate change at different ages and life stages [High Confidence]. For example, the very young and the very old are particularly sensitive to climate-related health impacts.

- Social Determinants of Health Interact with Climate Factors to Affect Health Risks

  Key Finding 3: Climate change threatens the health of people and communities by affecting exposure, sensitivity, and adaptive capacity [High Confidence]. Social determinants of health, such as those related to socioeconomic factors and health disparities, may amplify, moderate, or otherwise influence climate related health effects, particularly when these factors occur simultaneously or close in time or space [High Confidence].

- Mapping Tools and Vulnerability Indices Identify Climate Health Risks

---

[2] Dodgen, D., et al. (2016). Mental health and well-being. In USGCRP, *The impacts of climate change on human health in the United States: A scientific assessment* (pp. 217–246). Washington, DC: U.S. Global Change Research Program. Retrieved from http://dx.doi.org/10.7930/J0TX3C9H

Key Finding 4: The use of geographic data and tools allows for more sophisticated mapping of risk factors and social vulnerabilities to identify and protect specific locations and groups of people [High Confidence].[3]

Read&Write 8.1   Explore the Relationship of Climate Change to Mental Health

Your first task in this exercise is to read chapters 8 ("Climate Change and Mental Health") and 9 ("Populations of Concern") of the climate change impacts report published by the U.S. Global Change Research Program. Together, these two chapters identify many populations, using such defining factors as ethnicity, economic status, age, and occupation, that are particularly vulnerable to the effects of climate change. Your second task is to write a research paper in which you construct two "vulnerability profiles."

The first is your "Family Mental Health Vulnerability Profile." In this profile you will list the members of your immediate family, including yourself, and then write two paragraphs for each person in your list. In the first paragraph for each family member, you will describe the person by age, gender, occupation, health condition, disabilities, and other relevant factors, and you will note the state where each person lives. In the second paragraph for each family member, you will explain the factors identified in chapters 8 and 9 of the climate change report that apply to that person.

The second major component of your research paper is your "Family Geographic Vulnerability Profile." Employing information you find in chapter 9 of the climate change report, you will identify, for each listed family member, factors affecting his or her social (economic, ethnic), heat (temperature ranges), and location (coastal, desert, mountain) vulnerabilities.

Finally, write a conclusion in which you sum up your family's mental health vulnerabilities with reference to their social situations and geographic locations.

8.2   SENSATION AND PERCEPTION

Most psychology texts introduce their readers to sensation and perception as the product of biological processes (sight, hearing, taste, touch, smell). One of the most effective pathways for understanding and even magnifying the powers of one's biological capacities is art. Few deny the well-researched psychological benefits of seeing a first-class movie, listening to music, tasting an exceptional meal, feeling the coolness of a pool on a hot summer day, or taking in the fragrance of spring's first red rose. For an example of the ways in which art may provide access to insights regarding sensation and perception, let's turn our analytical abilities to an exploration of the psychological treasures of ballet.

---

[3]   Gamble, J. L., et al. (2016). Populations of concern. In USGCRP, *The impacts of climate change on human health in the United States: A scientific assessment* (pp. 247–286). Washington, DC: U.S. Global Change Research Program. Retrieved from http://dx.doi.org/10.7930/J0Q81B0T

Ballet? Really? What does ballet have to do with psychology? If such questions have never occurred to you before, they will now. The authors of this manual expect that you will find this chapter section to be especially challenging—and rewarding. In addition to refining your reading and writing skills (and offering you a new appreciation for the value of dissertations as resources for research), the exercise below may leave you with an expanded awareness of potential avenues for insight in what some consider to be the outer boundaries of psychology, and an activated sense of the life-enriching value in seeing the world through a psychological lens.

Read & Write 8.2 Discover Movement and Depth in Art

In 2013 Maral Sultanian, a doctoral student at the Pacifica Graduate Institute, submitted a dissertation titled "Martha Graham Engages the Body and Its Dances as a Path into the Unconscious."[4] Written to complete her PhD in depth psychology, Ms. Sultanian's dissertation takes us beyond the physical fundamentals of biology to the therapeutic insights available in not only experiencing art but in applying analytical observation skills to it as well.

Your tasks in this exercise are to:

Download this dissertation from your college library's online catalog.

Write an analytical reflection in which you answer the questions listed in the table below, finding relevant material by reading the dissertation chapters in which the answers may be found or from which they may be generated.

Chapter Title	Task
Chapter 1 Introduction	What generated the author's interest in the topic?
	What was the author's predisposition to the topic?
	How is this topic relevant to psychology?
Chapter 2 Literature Review	Who were the founding investigators into the unconscious, and what were a few of their major discoveries?
	What insights have been gained about understanding the unconscious through dance?
	How does dance express itself as symbolic imagery?
	What has Martha Graham contributed to dance and, especially, to dance as symbolic imagery?
	What are Carl Jung's major contributions to understanding the unconscious?
	What is the need for research on this topic in psychology?
	In what ways are psychology and the arts reciprocally informative?

---

[4] Sultanian, M. P. (2013). *Martha Graham engages the body and its dances as a path into the unconscious* (Doctoral dissertation). Retrieved from http://pqdtopen.proquest.com/doc/1500558568.html?FMT=AI

	In what ways does empathic reflection of body movement enhance the therapeutic process?
Chapter 3 Statement of Research Question	What is the research question for this study?
Chapter 4 Methodology, Research Approach, and Procedures	What methodology is employed, and what are its advantages and limitations?
Chapter 6 Three Choreographies Presented in Written Form	Read one of the three choreographies and their analyses. What insights contained therein help you understand yourself and your life?

9

BECOMING OURSELVES

9.1   DEVELOPMENTAL PSYCHOLOGY

Wonder whatever happened to that "cool" kid you always envied in high school? Well, maybe she or he is not doing as well now as you may think. In the abstract to a 2014 article titled "What Ever Happened to the 'Cool' Kids? Long-Term Sequelae of Early Adolescent Pseudomature Behavior," University of Virginia psychologists Joseph P. Allen, Megan M. Schad, Barbara Oudekerk, and Joanna Chango define the term "pseudomature behavior" as behavior in adolescence "ranging from minor delinquency to precocious romantic involvement," and hypothesize that "early adolescent pseudomature behavior predicted long-term difficulties in close relationships, as well as significant problems with alcohol and substance use, and elevated levels of criminal behavior."[1]

Before examining the substantial findings of "What Ever Happened to the 'Cool' Kids?" it may be helpful to view neuroscientist Aditi Shankardass's TED Talk titled "A Second Opinion on Developmental Disorders." TED Talks' caption for Shankardass's presentations states:

> Developmental disorders in children are typically diagnosed by observing behavior, but Aditi Shankardass suggests we should be looking directly at brains. She explains how one EEG technique has revealed mistaken diagnoses and transformed children's lives.[2]

---

[1]   Allen, J. P., Schad, M. M., Oudekerk, B., & Chango, J. (2014, September–October). What ever happened to the "cool" kids? Long-term sequelae of early adolescent pseudomature behavior. *Child development, 85*(5), 1866–1880. doi:10.1111/cdev.12250

[2]   Shankardass, A. (2009, November). A second opinion on developmental disorders. *TED.* Retrieved from http://www.ted.com/talks/aditi_shankardass_a_second_opinion_on_learning_disorders

Read & Write 9.1   Explore the Perils of Pseudomaturity

This is an opportunity to fully engage in psychology scholarship by writing an article critique. First, watch "A Second Opinion on Developmental Disorders" at http://www.ted .com. Then, download a copy of "What Ever Happened to the 'Cool' Kids?" from your college online library, or obtain it through interlibrary loan. Highlight the article's major points as you read it. Following the directions in section 6.2 of this manual ("Critique an Academic Article"), write an article critique. In the conclusion to your critique explain what contribution, if any, brain imaging may be able to make to the problems stemming from pseudomaturity.

9.2   MOTIVATION AND EMOTION

It may be obvious that a person's motivations are influenced by his or her emotions. But in what ways are they influenced? Psychologists are working to understand the connections between motivation and emotion, and they are continually discovering new insights that add understanding—and, sometimes, confusion—to our grasp of human behavior.

Read & Write 9.2   Discover a Diary of Anger, Sadness, and Fear

Two PBS podcasts offer an enlightening introduction to the topic of the relationship between emotions and motivation. The first is a *NOVA* segment titled "The Deciding Factor," by David Levin. The *NOVA* caption for this program is

> Jennifer Lerner, a social psychologist at Harvard University, studies how emotions affect our financial decisions. In this podcast, hear about a new study she and her team are conducting that has revealed, among other things, how anger and sadness have very different effects on our economic choices.[3]

As you watch this podcast, make some notes about how anger and sadness may affect your financial choices.

The second *NOVA* program is "Is Fear Contagious?" by Anna Rothschild, who produces a program for PBS called *Gross Science* that investigates quirky facts uncovered by the sciences. Rothschild's *NOVA* program links viewers to a *Gross Science* episode presenting evidence that fear may actually spread from person to person like a virus.[4]

As you watch Rothschild's segment, make note of the ways you can spread fear and anxiety and how you may be susceptible to the fears and anxieties of others.

Your task in this exercise is twofold. First, for one week, write a daily "emotion diary." In this journal, make note of the times you experience fear, sadness, and anxiety each day.

---

[3]   Levin, D. (2010, March 1). The deciding factor. *NOVA*. Retrieved from http://www.pbs.org/wgbh/nova/body /emotions-decisions.html

[4]   Rothschild, A. (2017, February 16). Is fear contagious? *NOVA*. Retrieved from http://www.pbs.org/wgbh/nova /body/is-fear-contagious.html

You will probably find it helpful to make brief notations throughout the day and then, returning to them at day's end, write some observations about the circumstances and outcomes of each emotional experience.

Second, write an essay in which you describe (1) ways in which anger or sadness affected purchases or other financial decisions you made, and (2) times at which someone else's fear affected you or times at which, you suspect, your own fears affected someone else.

9.3 PERSONALITY

Know thyself.

The Oracle at Delphi's imperative for Socrates is the foundation of all psychology. It is the thread that binds together the discipline's academicians, who think they are psychology's only real social scientists, and its clinicians, who tend to think they individually do humanity more good in a single day than all the academicians put together. Yes, these are exaggerations, but the territorial disciplinary divisions within psychology today seem, at times, arrogant and discouraging. In truth, both groups make immense contributions to society, and it is a rare academic discipline that is not plagued by some sort of intellectual cleavage.

As with so many other explorations into various aspects of human culture, TED is a particularly good place to begin following the Oracle's advice. If you type "personality" into TED's search engine, you will encounter nine TED Talks in the "Who Are You?" playlist, all of which are to be found through the same URL: http://www .ted.com/playlists/354/who_are _you.

Read&Write 9.3 Know Thyself

Although you will find interesting material in all nine segments, three are essential to this exercise. The titles and brief introductions to each provided on this site are as follows:

Julian Baggini: Is there a real you?

> What makes you, you? Is it how you think of yourself, how others think of you, or something else entirely? Philosopher Julian Baggini draws from philosophy and neuroscience to give a surprising answer.[5]

Brian Little: Who are you, really? The puzzle of personality

> What makes you, you? Psychologists like to talk about our traits, or defined characteristics that make us who we are. But Brian Little is more interested in moments when we transcend those traits—sometimes because our culture demands it of us, and sometimes because we demand it of ourselves. Join Little as he dissects the surprising differences between introverts and extroverts and explains why your personality may be more malleable than you think.[6]

[5] Baggini, J. (November 2011). Is There a Real You? *TED*. Retrieved from https://www.ted.com/talks/julian _baggini_is_there_a_real_you

[6] Little, B. (2016, February). Who are you, really? The puzzle of personality. *TED*. Retrieved from http://www.ted .com/playlists/354/who_are_you

Dan Gilbert: The psychology of your future self

"Human beings are works in progress that mistakenly think they're finished." Dan Gilbert shares recent research on a phenomenon he calls the "end of history illusion," where we somehow imagine that the person we are right now is the person we'll be for the rest of time. Hint: that's not the case.[7]

Your objectives in this exercise are (1) to better understand yourself and (2) to find help for intentionally creating the self you wish to become, if you choose to do so. Begin by watching the three presentations and taking notes. If your notes are sufficiently detailed, you should be able to answer the following questions:

- What is Baggini's central argument?
- What is Baggini's central metaphor for what our personalities actually are?
- According to Baggini, how do you discover your true self?
- According to Little, what does the word "ocean" signify?
- According to Little, what are our three natures?
- According to Little, what is the correct ranking order for the frequency of sex experienced each month by the following four groups: extroverted women, introverted women, extroverted men, and introverted men? What point is Little trying to make by providing this information?
- According to Little, what factor actually indicates the manner in which you are different from other people?
- What does Gilbert mean by the "end of history illusion"?
- According to Gilbert, what mistake do we all too often make?

Your final task in this exercise is to write an essay in which, following the advice of Baggini, Little, and Gilbert, you construct three "portraits" of yourself:

1. The person you were five (or 10) years ago.
2. The person you are today.
3. The person you hope to create by five (or 10) years from now.

For items 1 and 3 above, consult with perhaps three or four friends and relatives. Ask them to describe your personality from five years ago and as it is today, and ask them if they think you have changed over that time. For item 3, imagine you are in the perfect occupation five or 10 years from now. Describe the place and your activity. Are you on a voyage to Mars? Are you helping establish a hospital in Uganda? Are you making pastries in the White House? Are you the Pope? Whatever you imagine you might be, ask yourself what personality characteristics you may need to be successful and fulfilled, and how you may develop the ones you lack.

---

[7] Gilbert, D. (2014, March). The psychology of your future self. *TED*. Retrieved from https://www.ted.com/talks/dan_gilbert_you_are_always_changing

9.4 SOCIAL PSYCHOLOGY

Social psychologist Jonathan Haidt is currently Thomas Cooley Professor of Ethical Leadership at New York University's Stern School of Business. In his TED talk, "The Moral Roots of Liberals and Conservatives," Haidt presents a five-part "toolbox" that he believes identifies the psychological foundations of fundamental moral differences between liberals and conservatives. But his ideological analysis is less important than its behavioral application. Making an elegant plea for moral humility, he asks each of us to step back from our personal political-ethical matrices to take a broader view, one that he believes may temper ideological extremes.[8]

Read&Write 9.4 Reflect on the Psychological Foundations of Ideology

Respond to Haidt. First, take notes while you watch "The Moral Roots of Liberals and Conservatives." Second, identify yourself as leaning toward liberal or conservative social values as Haidt defines them. Third, for the purpose of completing this exercise, allow yourself, for some moments at least, to "buy" Haidt's argument by adopting his "moral humility."

Finally, write a reflective essay in which you respond to situations noted in the three news items below, all typical items taken from the *New York Times*. For each news article, write three paragraphs. In the first, applying your personal liberal or conservative matrix, (1) define the cause of the problem identified in the article and (2) propose a public policy solution. Your second paragraph is your conception of the cause of and the solution to the problem at hand if you adopt Haidt's prescription for moral humility. In your third paragraph, compare your "ideological" analysis to Haidt's approach, evaluating the strengths and weaknesses of both.

Article 1: Dan Bilefsky, Stephen Castle, and Prashant S. Rao, "'We Are Not Afraid,' Theresa May Proclaims After U.K. Parliament Attack" (March 23, 2017) Describing an event in which a "terrorist" killed three people and wounded 40 others as he drove over sidewalks on his path to Britain's Parliament building, this article states:

> The Islamic State claimed responsibility on Thursday for the deadly attack outside the British Parliament, as Prime Minister Theresa May described the assailant as a British-born man whom the country's domestic intelligence agency had investigated for connections to violent extremism. . . . May said Thursday morning that the attacker was "a peripheral figure" who had been examined by MI5, Britain's domestic counterintelligence agency, but who had not been "part of the current intelligence picture."[9]

[8] Haidt, J. (2008, March). The moral roots of liberals and conservatives. *TED*. Retrieved from http://www.ted.com/talks/jonathan_haidt_on_the_moral_mind

[9] Bilefsky, D., Castle, S., & Prashant, S. R. *New York Times* News Service. (2017, March 23). "We are not afraid," Theresa May proclaims after U.K. Parliament attack. *Kentucky Standard*. Retrieved from http://www.kystandard.com/content/'we-are-not-afraid'-theresa-may-proclaims-after-parliament-attack

Article 2: Angus Deaton, "It's Not Just Unfair: Inequality Is a Threat to Our Governance" **(March 20, 2017)** In this review of Ganesh Sitaraman's book *The Crisis of the Middle-Class Constitution: Why Economic Inequality Threatens Our Republic*, Deaton writes:

> President Obama labeled income inequality "the defining challenge of our time." But why exactly? . . . Ganesh Sitaraman argues that the contemporary explosion of inequality will destroy the American Constitution, which is and was premised on the existence of a large and thriving middle class. . . . Jefferson was proud of his achievement in . . . writing the laws that "laid the ax to the root of Pseudoaristocracy."[10]

Article 3: Donna De La Cruz, "Why Kids Shouldn't Sit Still in Class" (March 21, 2017) In this article, Donna De La Cruz contrasts two views of increasing physical activity in the classroom:

> Sit still. It's the mantra of every classroom. But that is changing as evidence builds that taking brief activity breaks during the day helps children learn, . . . and a growing number of programs designed to promote movement are being adopted in schools. . . . But not all districts are embracing the trend of movement breaks. . . . "With only six and a half hours during the day, our priority is academics," said Tom Hernandez, the director of community relations for the Plainfield School District in Illinois.[11]

9.5 ABNORMAL PSYCHOLOGY

One of America's obsessions is violence. Gangs, terrorism, domestic violence, and other destructive behaviors continue to flourish despite society's best efforts to eradicate them. The current status of research into the causes and prediction of violence is preliminary at best. Much of the focus is centered on mental illness, and even if this research manages to answer some questions, other problems will no doubt remain, including:

How do we detect appropriate cases of relevant mental illnesses?

What about people without any history of relevant mental illness who commit violent acts?

If we find neurological links to violence in people without relevant mental illnesses, how do we detect people with these links in the population?

If a relevant factor in most human activity is opportunity, how do we limit opportunities such as access to semiautomatic weapons?

---

[10] Deaton, A. (2017, March 20). It's not just unfair: Inequality is a threat to our governance. *New York Times*. Retrieved from https://www.nytimes.com/2017/03/20/books/review/crisis-of-the-middle-class-constitution-ganesh-sitaraman-.html

[11] De La Cruz, D. (2017, March 21). Why kids shouldn't sit still in class. *New York Times*. Retrieved from https://www.nytimes.com/2017/03/21/well/family/why-kids-shouldn't-sit-still-in-class.html

Read&Write 9.5 Explore the Psychology of Violence

Sponsored by PBS, a *NOVA* program titled "Neuroscience of Violence" offers a brief overview of research into the causes of violent behavior. The PBS online summary of the video states:

> While there is some evidence linking violence in general to risk factors such as age, sex, substance abuse, and personality traits such as anger and impulsiveness, over many years, researchers have established that only a very small subset of people suffering from mental illness are likely to commit violent acts. NOVA investigates what we know and what we don't about the neuroscience of violence.[12]

More substantial coverage of the research done on the roots of violence is offered in an article titled "Neurocriminology: Implications for the Punishment, Prediction and Prevention of Criminal Behaviour," published in 2014 in *Nature Reviews Neuroscience.* The article's authors, University of Alabama psychologist Andrea Glenn and University of Pennsylvania psychologist Adrian Raine, conclude by making a guarded but disturbing claim:

> Neurocriminological research in particular, and neuroscience in general, are not yet poised to make immediate changes in the prediction, prevention and punishment of criminal offenders. . . . At the same time, notwithstanding difficulties in determining causality, there is increasing convergence from different disciplinary perspectives that neurobiological influences partly predispose an individual to offending.[13]

What the state of research boils down to, then, is that while we are still far from conclusive discoveries that point the way to solutions, sufficient evidence of neurobiological factors related to violence exists to support further research. In their substantial article, Glenn and Raine discuss major venues of neurocriminological research, including genetics, prenatal and perinatal influences, hormones and neurotransmitters, psychophysiology, brain imaging, and neurology. They also include discussions of the legal context of neurobiology and prospects for intervention and prevention.

Your tasks in this exercise are to:

1. View *NOVA*, "Neuroscience of Violence."
2. Read "Neurocriminology: Implications for the Punishment, Prediction and Prevention of Criminal Behaviour," which is available online from the University of Pennsylvania Center for Neuroscience & Sociology and may be downloaded here: http://repository.upenn.edu/neuroethics_pubs/109/
3. From "Neurocriminology," answer the question posed in the final sentence in "Box 2. Ventral Prefrontal Dysfunction, Pedophilia, and Legal Responsibility": "In the face of the order in which events occurred, was Michael responsible for his inappropriate sexual behavior with his stepdaughter?"

[12] Neuroscience of violence. (2012, December 21). *NOVA.* Retrieved from http://www.pbs.org/video/2320074486
[13] Glenn, A. L., & Raine, A. (2014). Neurocriminology: Implications for the punishment, prediction and prevention of criminal behaviour. *Nature Reviews Neuroscience, 15,* 54–63. Retrieved from http://dx.doi.org/10.1038/nrn3640

4. Now return to "Box 1. Genetics and the Intergenerational Transmission of Violence" and answer a similar question: "In the face of the obvious genetic (and possibly environmental) influences, was Jeffrey Landrigan responsible for the murders he committed?"

5. Write an essay in which you answer these questions, supporting your answers with information from Glenn and Raine's article.

6. As you read the article you will notice that neurocriminology as a scientific endeavor is laden with an array of moral implications. Identify three additional important moral questions inherent to this discipline and explain their appropriate roles in future research.

10

FUNDAMENTALS OF
PSYCHOLOGICAL SCIENCE

10.1 EXPERIMENTAL PSYCHOLOGY

The Fundamentals of Scientific Inquiry in the Discipline of Psychology

Psychology is an empirical science. This means that psychologists seek knowledge by accepting as true only those statements that are supported by evidence and that can be tested in scientific experiments. To discover a new fact or truth, psychologists first construct a *hypothesis*, a statement that defines a relationship between two variables, and then they collect evidence to determine whether the hypothesis is true. *Variables* are things that affect or are affected by other things. While a chemist may be interested in the relationship between such variables as temperature and oxidation, psychologists test variables of human cognition, emotion, and behavior, such as learning capacity, anger, stress, procrastination, aggression, or smoking. A psychologist's hypothesis, for example, might therefore be: "Smoking reduces stress," "Depression may be caused by lack of sunlight," or "Antisocial behavior may be diminished by establishing trust with authority figures."

To test hypotheses, psychologists often use *experiments*, controlled situations that allow researchers to determine the relationship between two variables by eliminating the effects of other variables. For example, an experimenter who wants to determine the effect of noise on levels of anxiety could measure the levels of anxiety of a selected group of people and then either increase or decrease the noise level to which the people are subjected, and finally measure the level of anxiety again. During this process, however, the experimenter will need to eliminate other variables that may affect the subjects' anxiety level, such as delays in beginning the experiment or prolonged disruptive influences during the experiment.

Psychologists have specific names for the variables within an experiment. The variable that is being affected (in our example, the subjects' level of anxiety) is the *dependent variable.* The variable creating the effect (the noise level) is the *indepen-dent variable.* *Control variables* are those variables that the experimenter wants to eliminate or control. Control variables may be either *antecedent variables,* which occur before the independent variable is applied (such as delays in starting the exper-iment), or *intervening variables,* which occur after the independent variable has been introduced (for example, disturbances during the experiment).

Experiments have produced a vast store of knowledge for psychologists. Con-sider two famous examples. In 1901 Russian psychologist Ivan Pavlov (1849–1936) conducted an experiment demonstrating that dogs could be made to salivate by ringing a bell. In his experiment, he first repeatedly gave dogs food at the sound of a bell and then eventually he rang the bell without offering food. When the dogs heard the bell, they began to salivate in anticipation of the food, even though no food was offered. This experiment led to Pavlov's development of the concept of *classical conditioning.*[1] In other experiments Pavlov demonstrated that classical con-ditioning also applies to people in a multitude of ways. For example, a person who in childhood once ate too much butter and became ill may throughout life begin to feel nauseated at the thought of butter. This person has been "conditioned" to dislike butter.

A second example of an experiment is drawn from the work of Yale professor Stanley Milgram. In a controversial experiment conducted in the early 1960s, Mil-gram proved that normally ethical people could be induced to comply with immoral demands by authority figures. Volunteers in Milgram's experiments were told to give other people painful electrical shocks as punishment for making mistakes in assigned tasks. The volunteers were unaware that the recipients of the shocks were actually confederates (people who assist in experiments, following the experiment-er's directions) and that, in reality, no actual voltage shocks were being delivered. Even though the volunteers believed their victims were in extreme pain, most of them continued to administer the shocks simply because they were urged to do so by authority figures. Of 40 volunteers, only five refused to deliver the most painful shocks. Another interesting fact is that not one of the volunteers reported the nature of the experiments to the university.[2] Milgram's experiment provided researchers with disturbing data about the complex relationship between the human tendency to obey authority and the needs of the human conscience.

Eliminating *extraneous* (unwanted) *variables* from an experiment is almost always a difficult task. What has become known as the *Hawthorne effect* is a famous exam-ple of how control variables can affect an experiment's results. In an early effort to improve employee productivity, in 1927 the Western Electric Company conducted experiments to determine if better lighting increased employee morale. To their surprise, the experimenters found that morale improved when they either increased or decreased the amount of light available to employees. What they discovered after further investigation was that the employees responded not to changes in light but to the fact that management cared about morale enough to test changes in their environment. Because employees interpreted the experiment as a sign of concern

---

[1] For a more detailed discussion of classical conditioning, see this article: Pavlov's dogs and classical con-ditioning. (n.d.). *Psychologist World.* Retrieved from https://www.psychologistworld.com/behavior /pavlov-dogs-classical-conditioning
[2] A fuller account of Stanley Milgram's experiment can be found in McLeod, S. (2007). The Milgram experiment. *SimplyPsychology.* Retrieved from https://www.simplypsychology.org/milgram.html

for their welfare, the very fact that an experiment was being conducted became an intervening variable in the study! The Hawthorne effect is one of the most famous of phenomena known generally as *experimenter effects*, or things that experimenters may do that inadvertently affect the results of an experiment.[3]

In addition to experimenter effects, psychologists must consider the ethical implications of their actions. Before conducting experiments, students should visit the American Psychological Association (APA) web page titled *Ethical Principles of Psychologists and Code of Conduct*. Clicking on the web page's "General Principles" subheading reveals five principles that govern the Code together with descriptions of those principles, which read, in part:

A. Beneficence and Nonmaleficence

   Psychologists strive to benefit those with whom they work and take care to do no harm . . . [and to] safeguard the welfare and rights of those with whom they interact.

B. Fidelity and Responsibility

   Psychologists establish relationships of trust . . . [and] uphold professional standards of conduct.

C. Integrity

   Psychologists seek to promote accuracy, honesty and truthfulness in the science, teaching and practice of psychology.

D. Justice

   Psychologists recognize that fairness and justice entitle all persons to access to and benefit from the contributions of psychology.

E. Respect for People's Rights and Dignity

   Psychologists respect the dignity and work of all people, and the rights of individuals to privacy, confidentiality, and self-determination.[4]

Read&Write 10.1 Write an Experimental Research Paper

Writing an experimental research paper requires the researcher to complete six basic tasks:

1. Define a problem or issue.
2. Develop a testable hypothesis.
3. Design the experiment.
4. Conduct the experiment.
5. Analyze the data.
6. Report the findings.

Step 1: Define a Problem or Issue The world is full of problems and issues of interest to psychologists. You may find them in your own or your friends' behaviors, in newspapers, on

---

[3] Shuttleworth, M. (2009, October 10). Hawthorne effect. *Explorable*. Retrieved from https://explorable.com /hawthorne-effect

[4] Ethical principles of psychologists and code of conduct: Including 2010 and 2016 amendments. (n.d.). American Psychological Association. Retrieved from http://www.apa.org/ethics/code/index.aspx

television, at the supermarket, or at the bowling alley. The key to a highly successful experimental research paper is to study something that interests you. An excellent way to find a good topic is to select a particular day of the week on which to be particularly observant of the world around you. Take notes at every possible moment during the day. Notice the simple things going on around you. Make observations. Your list might include entries that look something like this:

My roommate Janice always brushes her teeth with exactly 32 strokes of the toothbrush.

When the plane lands, all the passengers immediately stand up in the aisles, even though they always have to wait at least 10 minutes before the door opens.

Professor Sanchez gives excellent lectures, but she always mispronounces my name. I'm Jennifer, not Hennifer.

The librarian refuses to make change for the copy machine.

The vice president used the word "impact" 33 times in his presentation.

Garth blows smoke rings out his nose.

Jerry likes hip-hop rock music. I like blues and slow jazz.

Jerry likes the bright lights of Times Square. I like the soft tones of summer in Central Park.

After taking notes for a while, you may find that you are naturally interested in people's preferences in music and their reactions to colors. You wonder, "Can music influence a person's choice of colors?"

Step 2: Develop a Testable Hypothesis   As we noted previously, a hypothesis is a statement that defines a relationship between two variables. Continuing with our example, you might form an initial hypothesis:

Color preferences are affected by music.

This statement has the basic elements of a good hypothesis. It has a dependent variable (color preferences) and an independent variable (music). But this hypothesis is actually too broad. As it is stated, it covers all people, places, and times. Proving this hypothesis is too much for an elementary experiment. You then try to narrow the hypothesis as follows, so that you can realistically construct an experiment that might test it:

Research subjects exposed to hard rock music will tend to select bright and strong colors, whereas research subjects exposed to easy-listening music will be more likely to select soft, dull, or dark colors.

This hypothesis appears to be testable in a modest experiment.

Step 3: Design the Experiment   Experiments may be designed in dozens of ways, and you will need to consult with your instructor to determine if your design is appropriate for your hypothesis. Many simple experiments, however, will follow the procedures described in our example. To design your experiment you will need to:

- Select subjects.

- Establish experimental and control groups.
- Design the experimental activity.
- Design the data collection and analysis procedures.

To generate results that reflect patterns in the general population, you would need to conduct a random sample. Random sample procedures vary according to the project, and if you decide to conduct one, your instructor will give you specific instructions. For the purposes of an introductory exercise in experimentation, a *convenience sample*, which uses subjects easily available, is adequate. It will probably be most convenient to have your fellow psychology classmates be your subjects if your experiment concerns other people. If your class is to be your sample population, an easy way to divide it into groups randomly is to write the students' names on pieces of paper and draw them out of a hat, selecting every other name for your experimental and control groups, respectively.

Your experimental activity must clearly test your hypothesis. Since in our example we want to see if choice of music affects choice of color, our experimental design will involve three groups of students. We shall have them meet at the same time in three different rooms. All students will be provided identical sets of crayons (two bright, two light, two medium, two dull, and two dark) and a sheet of paper. All three groups will be given 10 minutes to draw a picture. Since different subjects for the pictures (for example, vacation, family, weather) may generate different emotions for different people, all three groups will be asked to draw their own interpretation, in color, of a black-and-white photograph of a country town in France. While each group is drawing, hard rock music will be played for the first group, easy-listening music for the second group, and no music at all for the third group.

To analyze the data, we shall minimize differing interpretations by having one person (the student conducting the experiment) analyze all the pictures. For each drawing, the student will estimate the percentage of the drawing that has utilized bright colors and the percentage of the drawing that has utilized soft colors. The student researcher will then construct a data presentation table that includes the items shown in the following table. Please note that this table provides only for calculating some basic statistics, including the ones described in section 2 of this chapter. Consult your instructor for directions concerning which statistics to use for your experiment and how to calculate them.

TABLE 10.1

| Predominant Color Group in Each Drawing | Numbers of Participants in Each Music or No Music Group | | | |
	Hard Rock Listeners	Easy-Listening Listeners	No Music Participants	Total Participants
Bright				
Light				
Medium				
Dull				
Dark				
Total Drawings				

Step 4: Conduct the Experiment   Follow your research design (like the one above) as carefully as possible in conducting your experiment. In this case, for example, the rooms utilized should be identical for the three participant groups.

Note: Most colleges and universities have policies concerning research with human subjects, even in classroom activities. Sometimes a college or university will establish the administrative office known as the *institutional review board* (IRB) to review research proposals to ensure that the rights of human subjects are protected. It may be necessary for you to obtain permission, either from such a board or from your college, to conduct your experiment. *Be sure to comply with all policies of your university with respect to research with human subjects.*

Step 5: Analyze the Data   Your data analysis techniques should carefully follow your research design. In the case of our example experiment, you would first complete the table above. Then, using the statistical measures discussed in section 10.2 or other statistical measures recommended by your instructor, complete your data analysis.

Step 6: Report the Findings   Reporting your findings involves three tasks. First, state the *statistics* produced by your data analysis. Second, carefully state the *results* of the statistics. This statement entails posing and then answering the question, "To what extent do the statistics generated by this experiment support the hypothesis of the experiment?" Restate your hypothesis, which, in this example, is

Research subjects exposed to hard rock music will tend to select bright and strong colors, whereas research subjects exposed to easy-listening music will be more likely to select soft colors.

Your answer to this question will assert a certain type of relationship between hard rock music and bright and strong colors, and the strength of the statistical significance will allow you to categorize the relationship as low, medium, high, or negative. Here is a selection of possible responses you might make:

- "There is a high correlation between hearing hard rock music and the appearance of bright and strong colors in participant drawings."
- "There is a medium correlation between hearing hard rock music and the appearance of bright and strong colors in participant drawings."
- "There is a low correlation between hearing hard rock music and the appearance of bright and strong colors in participant drawings."
- "There is a negative correlation between hearing hard rock music and the appearance of bright and strong colors in participant drawings."

Your third task is to *discuss* your results by assessing the implications of the results. You may make statements such as these:

- "Hard rock music *produces* bright and strong colors in participant drawings."
- "Hard rock music *sometimes produces* bright and strong colors in participant drawings."
- "Hard rock music *occasionally produces* bright and strong colors in participant drawings."
- "Hard rock music *reduces* bright and strong colors in participant drawings."
- "The data are not statistically significant, and therefore no conclusion about the relationship between music and color preference may be drawn."

Your discussion section can then carefully posit other implications of your results and suggest opportunities for further research. You may write, for example, something like this:

Hard rock music appears to affect the emotional status of people. It would be interesting to know how it affects people in various other activities such as playing tennis, truck driving, hair styling, making cookies, serving on a departmental hiring committee, filing for divorce, jumping off a bridge, playing ping-pong with Paul Ryan, moving to Cape Breton Island, conducting plastic surgery, inspecting nuclear facilities, or operating military drones.

Elements of an Experimental Research Paper According to the guidelines established by the APA, experimental research papers are composed of five basic elements, the textual elements of which correspond to the activities described above:

1. Title Page
2. Abstract
3. Text
   a. Introduction
   b. Literature
   c. Methods
   d. Results
   e. Discussion
4. Reference Page
5. Appendices

As your project proceeds, consult the information given in previous chapters of this manual about how to research, structure, draft, revise, and format a research paper, and conduct your data analysis by using the statistical measures in section 10.2 below or other statistical measures recommended by your instructor.

10.2 STATISTICS FOR PSYCHOLOGY

Psychologists continually conduct a wide array of experiments. One of APA's many interesting web pages is titled "Particularly Interesting Experiments in Psychology" and offers, as its subtitle indicates, "Summaries of Research Trends in Experimental Psychology." On November 10, 2016, this page featured, among others, the following articles:

- "Mathematical and Spatial Abilities Are Strongly Related"
- "Sentence Context Influences Reading"
- "Western Diets Influence Behavior via the Hippocampus"
- "Inferring Trust from Explicit and Implicit Behavior"[5]

---

[5] Particularly exciting experiments in psychology. (n.d.). American Psychological Association. Retrieved from http://www.apa.org/pubs/highlights/peeps

At the APA website (http://www.apa.org) you will find information about many other research projects. These studies use statistical measures in their data analyses, most of which are common to all the social sciences. Statistics help research psychologists to determine how accurate and predictive their findings are. Varieties of statistics abound, as you will discover in your experimental psychology course. Since this chapter is an introduction to experimental psychology, we will stick with a few basic statistical measures, but first, let's see what some of our options might be if we were to conduct an experiment like the one discussed in section 10.1 of this chapter, but on a larger scale.

Let's suppose, for example, that we want to study the relationship of music to color preferences, but with a larger set of participants—420 people drawn from our college community as a whole and divided into several groups: men and women; age below 30 and age 30 and above; and whose major interest is in (1) science-based and technical fields, (2) education, (3) business, or (4) arts, social sciences, and humanities. Furthermore, we set our music selections at two different volume levels, medium-high and medium-low.

Let's look at a few options. Once we have gathered our data by conducting experiments like those described in section 10.1, we want to know the *variance*, that is, the spread of color preferences among some of our sample divisions. If we are testing the effects of a single independent variable—for example, the type of music played—we may want to perform an *ANOVA*, an Analysis of Variance between and among our groups. If we want to test the effects of two independent variables—type and volume of music—we may want to employ a *MANOVA*, a Multivariate Analysis of Variance, or a *regression*, which is good for testing the effects of one or more independent variables on a dependent variable.

Next, we may want to analyze *correlation* and *dependence*. To what extent, for example, is the selection of bright colors a function of hard rock music? One analysis option is the Pearson Product-Moment Correlation, which measures the dependence of one quantity upon another. Spearman's Rank Correlation Coefficient and Kendall's Rank Correlation Coefficient also measure the extent to which the strength of one variable is dependent upon another variable. When the music gets louder, how much does another variable rise or fall?

Read&Write 10.2 Calculate Statistical Significance

What about *statistical significance*, that is, how likely is it that your sample will accurately reflect the population as a whole? Pearson's χ^2 test is a good one for establishing statistical significance in a population with a normal population distribution (a bell-shaped curve).

For this exercise we have selected three statistical measures for you to employ in a simple, convenient sample experiment: a standard deviation, Tau c, and χ^2. We have *not* selected these three instruments because they are most commonly used or most effective for any particular type of experiment. We have selected them for two reasons:

1. They do provide helpful information about simple data sets.
2. They are relatively easy to manually (without a computer) calculate for small data sets. Therefore, we can encourage you, in the exercise below, to manually calculate the data for your own experiment using these statistical measures. Such a manual

calculation allows you to gain a deeper understanding of what statistics do and how they do it than if you simply analyze your raw data with a computer program.

Once again, consult with your instructor about selecting the best statistical measures for your own experiment.

We will now apply our selected statistical measures to the results of the experiment described in section 10.1 above.

Your experimental activity must clearly test your hypothesis. Since in our example we want to see if choice of music affects choice of color, our experimental design will involve three groups of students. We will have them meet at the same time in three different rooms. All students will be provided identical sets of crayons (two bright, two light, two medium, two dull, and two dark) and a sheet of paper. All three groups will be given 10 minutes to draw a picture. Since different subjects for the pictures (for example, vacation, family, weather) may generate different emotions for different people, all three groups will be asked to draw their own interpretation, in color, of a black-and-white photograph of a country town in France. While each group is drawing, hard rock music will be played for the first group, easy-listening music for the second group, and no music at all for the third group.

We shall minimize differing interpretations by having one person (the student conducting the experiment) analyze all the pictures. For each drawing, the student will estimate the percentage of the drawing that has utilized each of five types of colors: bright, light, medium, dull, and dark. The student researcher will then construct a data presentation table.

Predominant Color Group in Each Drawing	Numbers of Participants in Each Music or No Music Group			
	Hard Rock Listeners	Easy-Listening Listeners	No Music Participants	Total Participants
Bright				
Light				
Medium				
Dull				
Dark				
Total Drawings				

Forty-two participants will be divided into three groups in three identical conference rooms, with 14 participants in each room. Each participant will be provided a single sheet of white paper and the exact same 10 crayons in the following five pairs of colors:

- bright yellow and bright red
- light blue and light rose
- medium green and medium purple
- dull brown and dull gray
- dark brown and black

Participants will then be asked to draw a picture of anything they like for the next half hour. Group 1 will hear hip-hop and hard rock music. Group 2 will hear easy-listening and soft jazz music. Group 3 will hear no music at all.

Next, a color group assessor (a single person to eliminate multi-assessor bias) will divide all the drawings into five categories determined by the predominant color group found in each drawing. Each color group is assigned a point value and the following table is then constructed:

Predominant Color Group in Each Drawing	Point Value	Number of Drawings	Point Value Multiplied by Number of Drawings
Bright	1	8	8
Light	2	16	32
Medium	3	12	36
Dull	4	4	16
Dark	5	2	10
Total		42	102
Mean			2.43

As you can see, the predominant colors were bright in eight drawings, the predominant colors were light in 16 drawings, and so forth. We can see that there are 42 total drawings and 102 total value points. Dividing the number of value points (102) by the total number of drawings (42), we get a mean of 2.43. The *mean* is a mathematical expression of what the table tells us. We can see from this very simple table that the predominant colors were either bright or light in 24 drawings and predominantly medium, dull, or dark in 18 drawings; therefore, one-quarter more drawings featured bright or light colors than featured medium, dull, or dark colors. If the predominant color selection in all drawings had been evenly distributed among the five color groups, the mean would have been 3. A mean of 2.43, which is less than 3, tells us that the drawings tend to feature bright and light colors more than the darker options.

A mean is a shorthand expression of a distribution of values that can be combined with other statistical values to produce single numbers that express complex relationships.

While a mean tells us how properties (e.g., color preferences) coalesce, we may also want to know the extent to which they disperse to the extremes of their qualities (bright to dark). A frequently used statistical measure of dispersion is the *standard deviation*, which provides a single number that indicates how dispersed the responses to a given question are. To calculate the standard deviation(s) for our set of color preferences, we will follow these steps:

1. Assign a value to each preference (bright, light, medium, dull, dark) and the frequency of each preference.
2. Find the mean for the preference.
3. Subtract the value from the mean for all pairs (2.43).
4. Square the results of step 3.
5. Multiply the results of step 4 by the frequency of each value.
6. Sum the values in step 5.
7. Divide the values in step 6 by the number of preferences.
8. Find the square root of the value in step 7, which is the standard deviation.

Step								
	1	2	3	4	5	6	7	8
Value	Frequency	Mean	Mean minus value	Step 3 squared	Step 4 times the frequency	Sum of values in Step 5	Step 6 divided by the total of frequencies (42)	Square Root of Step 7 = *Standard Deviation*
1	8	2.43	1.43	2.045	16.36	2	16	2.43
.43	.185	2.96	3	12	2.43	−.57	.325	3.90
4	4	2.43	−1.57	2.460	9.84	5	2	2.43
−2.57	6.600	13.20		42				
46.26	1.10	1.05						

The standard deviation of our question is 1.05. To understand its significance, we need to know that standard deviations compare the dispersion in a set of data to what is known as a *normal distribution*. In a normal distribution, 68.26 percent of the drawings will fall between (1) the mean minus one standard deviation (in our example, 2.43 − 1.05, or 1.38), and (2) the mean plus one standard deviation (in our example, 2.43 + 1.05, or 3.48). In other words, in a normal distribution, about two-thirds of the drawings in our experiment score between 1.38 and 3.48 on the standard deviation scale of assigned point values. Another one-third of the drawings will score less than 1.38 or more than 3.48.

For convenience, we shall call the extreme drawings bright and dark, and we shall designate light, medium, and dull as moderate drawings. We see that a score of 1.38 is closest to our first extreme, bright. A score of 3.48 inclines to the dull side of medium. We may conclude that a significant portion of the drawings (about one-quarter) tend to give extreme answers to our question. We may also notice that the score 1.38, which indicates strong agreement, is closer to its absolute extreme (1.38 is only .38 away from its absolute extreme of 1.0) than is the score 3.48 (which is 1.52 points from its absolute extreme of 5). This means that the drawings are slightly more tightly packed toward the extreme of strong agreement. We can now see more completely the degree of extremism in the pool of drawings.

Standard deviations become more helpful as the number of the elements in a study increases, because they allow us to compare quickly and easily the extent of extremism. You will find other measures of dispersion in addition to the standard deviation in your statistical methods textbooks.

After finding the amount of dispersion in responses to a question, you may want to see if different types of respondents answered the question in different ways—that is, you may want to measure *relationships* in the data. For example, examining our experimental and control group participants, we find 14 hard rock listeners, 14 easy-listening listeners, and 14 participants who don't listen to any sort of music. We shall call them hard rockers, easy listeners, and nonlisteners, respectively. To compare their preferences, we need to construct a *correlation matrix* that groups responses by the music to which they were exposed:

Color Emphasis	Hard Rockers	Easy Listeners	Nonlisteners	Total (Frequency)
Bright	3	2	2	7
Light	8	4	4	16
Medium	3	5	5	13
Dull	0	2	2	4
Dark	0	1	1	2

Each number of preferences in the matrix is found in a location known as a *preference cell*. The numbers in the Total (Frequency) column are known as *preference total cells*. From this matrix, it appears that hard rockers are more likely to use bright or light colors than are either easy listeners or nonlisteners. If this is true for the sample population, there is a *correlation* between music heard and choice of colors. How strong, however, is this correlation? The answer to this question may be gained by using a correlation measure, such as *Kendall's Tau c*, which is calculated by identifying pairs of preferences and matching the pairs according to a set formula. A *Tau c* is used when the number of rows is *not* the same as the number of columns (in other words, you have a rectangular data table such as the one in our example). Use a *Tau b* or other statistical measure provided by your statistics text or instructor if the number of columns and rows is identical.

To calculate a Tau c for the preferences in the correlation matrix above, the first step is to find the number of *concordant pairs* of preferences by multiplying the number of preferences in each cell in the correlation matrix by the numbers in the cells below and to the right. For example, we would multiply the number of bright preferences from hard rockers (3) by the sum of the numbers in preference cells (not preference total cells) below and to the right of the hard rockers column. Our calculation for this procedure would be as follows:

$$3(4 + 4 + 5 + 5 + 2 + 2 + 1 + 1)$$

We then repeat this procedure for every response in the response cells. When we have completed all possible operations of this type in the matrix, we add them together to obtain the number of concordant pairs (P):

$$3(4 + 4 + 5 + 5 + 2 + 2 + 1 + 1) + 2(4 + 5 + 2 + 1) + 8(5 + 5 + 2 + 2 + 1 + 1) +$$

$$4(5 + 2 + 1) + 3(2 + 2 + 1 + 1) + 5(2 + 1) + 0(1 + 1) + 2(1)$$

or

$$72 + 24 + 128 + 32 + 18 + 15 + 0 + 2 = 291. \text{ Therefore, } P = 291$$

Our next task is to calculate the number of *discordant pairs* (Q), which equals the total of the numbers in the cells above and to the right of each response. In our matrix above, there are no numbers above and to the right of the first number in the matrix (3), so we begin by multiplying the number 8 in the hard rockers, by the number in response cells (not response total cells) above and to the right of the hard rockers column. We then proceed to each other number in a cell in the same manner, skipping all cells in which no response number appears above and to the right.

Here again is our chart:

Color Emphasis	Hard Rockers	Easy Listeners	Nonlisteners	Total (Frequency)
Bright	3	2	2	7
Light	8	4	4	16
Medium	3	5	5	13
Dull	0	2	2	4
Dark	0	1	1	2

Our calculation would be as follows:

$$8(2+2)+4(2)+3(2+2+4+4)+5(2+4)+0(2+2+4+4+5+5)+2(2+4+5)$$
$$+0(2+2+4+4+5+5+2+2)+1(2+4+5+2)$$

or

$$32+8+36+30+0+22+0+13=141. \ Q, \text{ therefore, equals } 141.$$

Using the numbers we have obtained, we will now calculate the following formula:

$$\frac{P-Q}{\frac{1}{2}(N)^2 \left[(m-1)/m \right]}$$

where N = number of cases (42) and m = the smaller number of rows or columns (3).

The numbers for this formula that our example has yielded are as follows:

$$P = 291, Q = 141$$

$$\frac{P-Q}{\frac{1}{2}(N)^2 \left[(m-1)/m \right]}$$

$$\frac{150}{\frac{1}{2}(42)^2 \left[(3-1)/3 \right]}$$

$$\frac{150}{588} = 0.255$$

Our Tau c value is therefore .26. This value may now be interpreted. Tau c values range from +1.0, a number indicating a perfectly positive correlation between the variables tested (in our example, music and color brightness), to –1.0, a perfectly negative correlation between the two variables. A value of 0 would indicate no correlation at all. A positive correlation is a relationship in which one value is found when another is present. If, for example, flowers bloom after it rains, then there is a positive correlation between rainfall and the blooming of flowers. A negative correlation indicates the presence of one factor when another factor is absent. If flowers fail to bloom when it snows, then there is a negative correlation between flowers blooming and snow. Strong positive correlations have scores close to 1.0 (.8 or .9, for example). Strong negative correlations have scores close to –1.0 (–.8 or –.9, for example). Weak correlations have scores close to 0 (–.2 or .1, for example). In our example, the correlation between music and color preference is positive: .26. This is a relatively weak positive correlation. That is, people who draw while hearing hard rock music tend to use more bright colors, but not all hard rockers do. If in a study involving numerous interrelated factors, you calculate the Tau c values for a number of different relationships among your factors, you will be able to evaluate the *strength* of relationships among many factors.

The third type of statistical procedure that should be performed in analyzing experiments and other sorts of data is a measure of statistical significance. In the Tau c that we have just calculated, we found a .26 correlation between music and color preferences. How do we know if the results of our sample accurately represent the population from which they are drawn? The answer is that we must test the statistical significance of the data. The purpose of testing statistical significance is to determine the likelihood that our findings are not representative but merely the result of chance.

A chi-square (χ^2) is one commonly used measure of statistical significance. It may be calculated as described below, using this example:

Color Emphasis	Hard Rockers	Easy Listeners	Nonlisteners	Total (Frequency)
Bright	3	2	2	7
Light	8	4	4	16
Medium	3	5	5	13
Dull	0	2	2	4
Dark	0	1	1	2
Total	14	14	14	42

Notice the totals for each row and column. To calculate χ^2 we must first determine *expected* values for each category of response. This means that we must find out what values would occur in each cell if all responses were exactly proportional to the totals. We shall make up a new matrix, starting with the column and row totals, and fill it in not with the actual responses but with expected values instead.

To find the expected values, we multiply the row total by the column total and divide by the matrix total (the total number of preferences in our example above is 42). The expected values may be rounded to the closest whole number. To find the expected value for the cell for bright-coloring hard rockers, therefore, we multiply the row total in the chart above (7) by the column total (14) divided by the matrix total (42), which yields the result (3) when rounded up. We now continue the same process, filling in the expected values for each cell to arrive at the following matrix of expected values:

Color Emphasis	Hard Rockers	Easy Listeners	Nonlisteners	Total (Frequency)
Bright	3	3	3	9
Light	6	6	6	18
Medium	5	5	5	15
Dull	2	2	2	6
Dark	1	1	1	3
Total	17	17	17	51

The next step is to find the differences between expected and actual values. Within each cell, subtract the expected value from the actual value. In the cell for bright-coloring hard rockers, therefore, we subtract the expected value (3) from the actual number of responses for that cell (3), and our result is 0. Completing this calculation for each cell, we have the following table of the differences among expected and actual cell values:

Color Emphasis	Hard Rockers	Easy Listeners	Nonlisteners	Total (Frequency)
Bright	3 – 3 = 0	2 – 3 = –1	2 – 3 = –1	7
Light	8 – 6 = 2	4 – 6 = –2	4 – 6 = –2	16
Medium	3 – 5 = –2	5 – 5 = 0	5 – 5 = 0	13
Dull	0 – 2 = –2	2 – 2 = 0	2 – 2 = 0	4
Dark	0 – 1 = –1	1 – 1 = 0	1 – 1 = 0	2

And so:

Color Emphasis	Hard Rockers	Easy Listeners	Nonlisteners	Total (Frequency)
Bright	0	–1	–1	7
Light	2	–2	–2	16
Medium	–2	0	0	13
Dull	–2	0	0	4
Dark	–1	0	0	2

Our next step is to square the differences within each cell, which yields the results shown below:

Color Emphasis	Hard Rockers	Easy Listeners	Nonlisteners	Total (Frequency)
Bright	0	1	1	7
Light	4	4	4	16
Medium	4	0	0	13
Dull	4	0	0	4
Dark	1	0	0	2

Next, for each cell, we divide the squared difference values in the above matrix by the expected values, as shown below:

Color Emphasis	Hard Rockers	Easy Listeners	Nonlisteners	Total (Frequency)
Bright	0/3 = 0	1/3 = 0.33	1/3 = 0.33	7
Light	2/6 = 0.33	4/6 = 0.66	4/6 = 0.66	16
Medium	4/5 = 0.8	0/5 = 0	0/5 = 0	13
Dull	4/2 = 2	0/2 = 0	0/2 = 0	4
Dark	1/1 = 1	0/1 = 0	0/1 = 0	2

We next add up the values in the above matrix for a total of 6.13, which is the χ^2 value for our experiment. To use the value, however, we need two more pieces of information. First, we must determine the matrix's *degrees of freedom*, which is a statistical device that relates the number of response choices to the results of the experiment. To find the degrees of freedom in a matrix, proceed as follows:

1. Count the number of data (not total) columns in the matrix (in our case there are 3), and subtract 1. The result for our example is 2.
2. Count the number of data (not total) rows in the matrix (in our case there are 5), and subtract 1. The result for our example is 4.
3. Multiply these two numbers to obtain the degrees of freedom. The result for our example is 8.

Using the following table, we find the value corresponding to the degree of freedom for your matrix. If your χ^2 value exceeds the value in the table, then your result is statistically significant at the .05 level. This means that there are only five chances in 100 that the results of your experiment are not statistically significant.

Freedom	Value	Freedom	Value	Freedom	Value
1	3.8	11	19.7	21	32.7
2	6.0	12	21.0	22	33.9
3	7.8	13	22.4	23	35.2
4	9.5	14	23.7	24	36.4
5	11.1	15	25.0	25	37.7
6	12.6	16	26.3	30	43.8
7	14.1	17	27.6	40	55.8
8	15.5	18	28.9	50	67.5
9	16.2	19	30.1	60	79.1
10	18.3	20	31.4	70	90.5

Our results for our question show a χ^2 of 6.13 with 8 degrees of freedom. Our chart shows that we need a value of at least 15.5 for our data to be significant at the .05 level. Any value for our data higher than 15.5 would indicate that our results are significant, but our total is only 6.13. According to our χ^2 test, therefore, our data are not statistically significant. This is probably because our sample size is too small. You may well have the same result with your own experiment if you use your psychology class as your sample. We have used as an example a sample that is not statistically significant, and we encourage the use of classroom samples that may also not be statistically significant, for two reasons: First, the convenience and educational potential of using the classroom sample are substantial. Second, the purpose of writing your paper is to learn how to conduct and analyze an experiment; it is not necessary for your sample to be significant for you to gain this knowledge. It is perfectly acceptable, of course, to use a sample of sufficient size to secure statistical significance.

REFERENCES

About the book. (n.d.). *Singularity.com*. Retrieved from http://singularity.com/aboutthebook .html

Aging in America: Perspectives from psychological science. (2016, May–June). *American Psychologist*. Retrieved from http://www.apa.org/pubs/journals/special/4017105.aspx

Allen, J. P., Schad, M. M., Oudekerk, B., & Chango, J. (2014, September–October). What ever happened to the "cool" kids? Long-term sequelae of early adolescent pseudomature behavior. *Child development*, 85(5), 1866–1880. doi:10.1111/cdev.12250

Babb, D. (2014, September 5). LBJ's 1964 attack ad "Daisy" leaves a legacy for modern campaigns. *Washington Post*. Retrieved from https://www.washingtonpost.com/opinions/lbjs-1964-attack -ad-daisy-leaves-a-legacy-for-modern-campaigns/2014/09/05/d00e66b0-33b4-11e4 -9e92-0899b306bbea_story.html

Baggini, J. (November 2011). Is There a Real You? *TED*. Retrieved from https://www.ted.com /talks/julian_baggini_is_there_a_real_you

Balas, B., & Thomas, L. (2015). Competition makes observers remember faces as more aggressive. *Journal of Experimental Psychology*, 144(4), 711–716. doi:10.1037/xge0000078

Bilefsky, D., Castle, S., & Prashant, S. R., *New York Times* News Service. (2017, March 23). "We are not afraid," Theresa May proclaims after U.K. Parliament attack. *Kentucky Standard*. Retrieved from http://www.kystandard.com/content/'we-are-not-afraid'-theresa-may -proclaims-after-parliament-attack

Bowen, M. (1978). *Family therapy in clinical practice*. Northvale, NJ: Jason Aronson.

Bulwer-Lytton, E. (186-?). *Richelieu: Or, the conspiracy, a play in five acts*. In *Making of America*. New York, NY: Samuel French. Ann Arbor, MI: University of Michigan Library (2005). Retrieved from http://name.umdl.umich.edu/AAX3994.0001.001 (Original work published 1839)

d'Aquili, E., & Newberg, A. B. (1999). *The mystical mind: Probing the biology of religious experience*. Minneapolis, MN: Fortress.

Deaton, A. (2017, March 20). It's not just unfair: Inequality is a threat to our governance. *New York Times*. Retrieved from https://www.nytimes.com/2017/03/20/books/review/crisis -of-the-middle-class-constitution-ganesh-sitaraman-.html

De La Cruz, D. (2017, March 21). Why kids shouldn't sit still in class. *New York Times*. Retrieved from https://www.nytimes.com/2017/03/21/well/family/why-kids-shouldnt-sit-still-in -class.html

Dodgen, D., Donato, D., Kelly, N., La Greca, A., Morganstein, J., Reser, et al. (2016). Mental health and well-being. In A. Crimmins, J. Balbus, J. L. Gamble, C. B. Beard, J. E. Bell, D. Dodgen, et al., *The impacts of climate change on human health in the United States: A scientific assessment* (pp. 217–246). Washington, DC: U.S. Global Change Research Program. Retrieved from http://dx.doi.org/10.7930/J0TX3C9H.

Dr. Seuss. (1960). *Green eggs and ham*. New York, NY: Random House.

Ethical principles of psychologists and code of conduct: Including 2010 and 2016 amendments. (n.d.). American Psychological Association. Retrieved from http://www.apa.org/ethics /code/index.aspx

Forster, E. M. (1956). *Aspects of the novel*. New York, NY: Harvest. (Original work published 1927)

Gamble, J. L., Balbus, J., Berger, M., Bouye, K., Campbell, V., Chief, K., et al. (2016). Populations of concern. In A. Crimmins, J. Balbus, J. L. Gamble, C. B. Beard, J. E. Bell, D. Dodgen, et al., *The impacts of climate change on human health in the United States: A scientific assessment* (pp. 247–286). Washington, DC: U.S. Global Change Research Program. Retrieved from http://dx.doi.org/10.7930/J0Q81B0T

García-Vera, M. P., Sanz, J., & Gutiérrez, S. (2016, July). A systematic review of the literature on posttraumatic stress disorder in victims of terrorist attacks. *Psychological Reports, 119*(1), 328–359. doi:10.1177/0033294116658243

Gilbert, D. (2014, March). The psychology of your future self. *TED*. Retrieved from https://www.ted.com/talks/dan_gilbert_you_are_always_changing

Glenn, A. L., & Raine, A. (2014). Neurocriminology: Implications for the punishment, prediction and prevention of criminal behaviour. *Nature Reviews Neuroscience, 15*, 54–63. Retrieved from http://dx.doi.org/10.1038/nrn3640

Haidt, J. (2008, March). The moral roots of liberals and conservatives. *TED*. Retrieved from http://www.ted.com/talks/jonathan_haidt_on_the_moral_mind

Hartwell, P. (1985). Grammar, grammars, and the teaching of grammar. *College English, 47*, 105–127.

Health indicator report of drug overdose deaths. (2015, 2 November). *New Mexico's Indicator-Based Information System (NM-IBIS)*. Retrieved from http://ibis.health.state.nm.us

Johnson, G. (2016, July 4). Consciousness: The mind messing with the mind. *New York Times*. Retrieved from http://www.nytimes.com/2016/07/05/science/what-is-consciousness.html

Johnson, S. G., Rajeev-Kumar, G., & Keil, F. C. (2016). Sense-making under ignorance. *Cognitive Psychology, 89*, 39–70. doi:10.1016/j.cogpsych.2016.06.004

Kurzweil, R. (2005). *The singularity is near: When humans transcend biology*. New York, NY: Viking.

Lincoln, A. ([1863] n.d.). The Gettysburg address. *Abraham Lincoln Online*. Retrieved from http://www.abrahamlincolnonline.org/lincoln/speeches/gettysburg.htm

Levin, D. (2010, March 1). The deciding factor. *NOVA*. Retrieved from http://www.pbs.org/wgbh/nova/body/emotions-decisions.html

Little, B. (2016, February). Who are you, really? The puzzle of personality. *TED*. Retrieved from http://www.ted.com/playlists/354/who_are_you

Marlin, E. (1989). *Genograms*. Chicago, IL: Contemporary Books.

McGoldrick, M., & Gerson, R. (1986). *Genograms in family assessment*. New York, NY: Norton.

McLeod, S. (2007). The Milgram experiment. *SimplyPsychology*. Retrieved from https://www.simplypsychology.org/milgram.html

McLeod, S. (2008). Psychosexual stages. *SimplyPsychology*. Retrieved from https://www.simplypsychology.org/psychosexual.html

McLeod, S. (2009). Defense mechanisms. *SimplyPsychology*. Retrieved from https://www.simplypsychology.org/defense-mechanisms.html

McLeod, S. (2013). Sigmund Freud. *SimplyPsychology*. Retrieved from http://www.simplypsychology.org/Sigmund-Freud.html

Miranda, D., Blais-Rochette, C., Vaugon, Osman, M., & Arias-Valenzuela, M. (2015). Towards a cultural-developmental psychology of music in adolescence (p. 197). *Psychology of Music, 43*(2), 197–218. Retrieved from http://journals.sagepub.com/doi/full/10.1177/0305735613500700

Murphy, K. (2016, August 6). Do your friends actually like you? *New York Times*. Retrieved from http://nyti.ms/2aWZCjy

Neuroscience of violence. (2012, December 21). *NOVA*. Retrieved from http://www.pbs.org/video/2320074486

Particularly exciting experiments in psychology. (n.d.). American Psychological Association. Retrieved from http://www.apa.org/pubs/highlights/peeps

Pavlov's dogs and classical conditioning. (n.d.). *Psychologist World*. Retrieved from https://www.psychologistworld.com/behavior/pavlov-dogs-classical-conditioning

Pearce, C. O. (1958). *A scientist of two worlds: Louis Agassiz*. Philadelphia, PA: Lippincott.

Publication manual of the American Psychological Association (6th ed.) (2010). Washington, DC: American Psychological Association.

Richie, B. S., Fassinger, R., Linn, S. G., Johnson, J., Prosser, J., & Robinson, S. (1997, April). Persistence, connection, and passion: A qualitative study of the career development of highly achieving African American–Black and White women. *Journal of Counseling Psychology, 44*(2), 133–148. doi:10.1037/0022-0167.44.2.133

Rothschild, A. (2017, February 16). Is fear contagious? *NOVA.* Retrieved from http://www.pbs .org/wgbh/nova/body/is-fear-contagious.html

Schneider, S. (2016, March 18). The problem of AI consciousness. [Blog post]. *KurzweilAINetwork.* Retrieved from http://www.kurzweilai.net/the-problem-of-ai-consciousness

Sendak, M. (1963). *Where the wild things are.* New York, NY: Harper & Row.

Shankardass, A. (2009, November). A second opinion on developmental disorders. *TED.* Retrieved from http://www.ted.com/talks/aditi_shankardass_a_second_opinion_on _learning_disorders

Shuttleworth, M. (2009, October 10). Hawthorne effect. *Explorable.* Retrieved from https:// explorable.com/hawthorne-effect

Sonin, A. (2013, April 16). Heritage: Sigmund Freud met his greatest admirer Salvadore Dali at Primrose Hill Home. *Ham&High.* Retrieved from http://www.hamhigh.co.uk/news /heritage/heritage-sigmund-freud-met-his-greatest-admirer-salvadore-dali-at-primrose-hill -home-1-2016573

Stark, F. Introducing the Medicare Mental Health Modernization Act (extensions of remarks— March 23, 2007). 110th Cong., 1st Sess., 153 Cong. Rec. 72 (2007).

Sultanian, M. P. (2013). *Martha Graham engages the body and its dances as a path into the unconscious* (Doctoral dissertation). Retrieved from http://pqdtopen.proquest.com/doc/1500558568 .html?FMT=AI

Taub, A. (2016, July 12). A social reflex: Police and Blacks, seeing threat, close ranks. *New York Times.* Retrieved from https://www.nytimes.com/2016/07/13/us/police-shootings-race .html

USGCRP. (2016). *The impacts of climate change on human health in the United States: A scientific assessment.* Washington, DC: U.S. Global Change Research Program. Retrieved from http:// dx.doi.org/10.7930/J0R49NQX

Wick, D., & Abraham, M. (Producers), & Scott, T. (Director). (2001). *Spy game.* U.S.: Beacon Pictures.

INDEX

A

abstracts
  defined, 58
  example, 58–59
  as experimental research paper component, 140
AI (artificial intelligence), 89–90
American Psychological Association (APA)
  background, vii
  Ethical Principles of Psychologists and Code of Conduct, 136
  "Particularly Interesting Experiments in Psychology," 140–50
  Publication Manual of the American Psychological Association, 63
  research project information, 141
  See also APA style
anal stage, 84
analogies, 5–6
ANOVA (analysis of variance), 141
antecedent variables, 135
APA style
  defined, 63
  references in, 69–73
  text citations in, 63–69
  See also American Psychological Association
apostrophes
  defined, 36
  importance of, 37
  use of, 36–37
appendices
  defined, 62
  as experimental research paper component, 140
  as genogram paper component, 105
  material in, 62
Aristotle, 83, 86
article critique
  article selection in, 106
  components of, 107
  contribution to the literature, 108
  defined, 105
  evidence of thesis support, 107–8
  journal selection in, 106
  methods, 107
  overview, 105–6
  preparing to write, 106
  recommendation, 108
  thesis, 107
  writing, 107–8
artificial intelligence (AI), 89–90
attentive listening, 91
attentiveness, 91
audience
  considering, 34–35
  research paper, 114
authority, 25–26

B

Baggini, Julian, 128
becoming ourselves
  abnormal psychology, 131–33
  developmental psychology, 126–27
  motivation and emotion, 127–28
  personality, 128–29
  social psychology, 130–31
behavior
  patterns of, 86
  social, 92–94
  TED Talks on, 86–87
behaviorists, 86
bias-free writing, 27–28
bibliography
  compiling, 79
  working, 119–20
bills and resolutions
  citing, 68
  references, 75
biological psychology, 121–23
block quotations, 48
book references
  with author as editor, 71
  author of foreword or introduction, 71–72
  classical texts, 73
  editor or compiler as author, 71
  electronic books, 77
  group as author, 71
  multivolume work, 72–73
  one author, 70
  republished book, 72
  selection in multiauthor collection, 72
  signed article in reference book, 72
  subsequent editions, 72
  three or more authors, 70
  translated book, 71
  two authors, 70
  two works by same author, 71
  unsigned article in encyclopedia, 72
  untranslated book, 71
  work with no author given, 71
  See also references
book reviews
  applications of, 108–9
  criteria for, 110
  elements of, 109–10
  questions answered by, 108
  writing, 108–10
  writing exercise, 110

C

capitalization
  proper nouns, 36–37
  rules, 37–38
  titles, 38